100 IDEAS
FOR TEACHING PRIMARY
MATHEMATICS

CONTINUUM 100 IDEAS FOR THE EARLY YEARS SERIES

CONTINUUM ONE HUNDREDS SERIES

100 IDEAS
FOR TEACHING
PRIMARY
MATHEMATICS

Alan Thwaites

continuum

UNIVERSITY OF CHICHESTER

Continuum International Publishing Group
The Tower Building   80 Maiden Lane
11 York Road   Suite 704
London   New York, NY 10038
SE1 7NX

www.continuumbooks.com

© Alan Thwaites 2008

British Library Cataloguing-in-Publication Data
A catalogue record for this book is available from the British
Library.

ISBN: (paperback) 978 18470 6381 6

Library of Congress Cataloging-in-Publication Data
A catalog record for this book is available from the Library of
Congress.

Designed and typeset by Ben Cracknell Studios |
www.benstudios.co.uk

Printed and bound in Great Britain by Cromwell Press, Wiltshire

510·
7HW

CONTENTS

SECTION 2   **Investigations and longer activities**

SECTION 3   **Measures and time**

SECTION 4 Shape, space and design

ACKNOWLEDGEMENTS

Many thanks to Judith Thwaites for her patience, ideas, encouragement and proofreading.

The ideas in this book have been collected and used over a number of years, but many have been refreshed and tested further with the enthusiastic help and support of staff and pupils at Sandown School, Hastings.

The aim of this book is to provide a resource for teachers and support staff which will supplement and enhance the primary mathematics syllabus. It is hoped that users will be able to select activities which will fit alongside their scheduled syllabus as well as use some of the ideas as ongoing consolidation of previously covered areas.

Essentially, all the ideas have been used successfully in the primary classroom situation. There is an element of friendly competition in many, most encourage cooperation in pairs or groups and all are intended to be enjoyable. It is hoped that users will find among these ideas, many repeatable favourites of both the children and themselves.

MATHS COVERAGE

I have tried to include as wide a range from the common primary mathematics syllabus as possible but there is a weighting towards concepts of number. Confidence in the way numbers are used and work together breeds willingness and enthusiasm to investigate and create further. If the idea title does not give a clue to the area covered then there is a brief reference at the start of each entry.

DURATION

Almost half the ideas are suited to short sessions of activity, perhaps at the beginning or end of a lesson. However, they could be combined to provide a 'circus' of activities over a longer period of time. Many can be easily adapted for a longer session, if appropriate, and any short game can be played a number of times.

GROUP SIZE

Recommendations for group sizes are given for each idea but it will be seen that many suggest, simply, 'any'. Some activities will lend themselves more to a smaller group but this does not mean they cannot be adapted to a much larger number or even a whole class. Whereas it could be said that any idea will work better with adult supervision, very many of these activities can be largely self-sufficient after initial guidance.

DIFFERENTIATION

The great majority of the activities are adaptable within the primary age and ability range. Where this is unlikely to be possible, a recommendation towards a broad age group is given. Brief notes on differentiation possibilities are included.

RESOURCES

No elaborate resources are required for any of the ideas. Any equipment needed is likely to be found in the primary classroom. Some ideas require preparation but this involves very little time and effort and, once prepared, the materials can be used repeatedly. Most of the activities require little or no preparation at all.

Short number activities and games

Ideas 1–48 are ideal for lesson starters or early finishers. They can also be used within a 'circus' of activities for a longer period. All should be used in the context of enjoyment and fun. Many of the games could be particularly suitable for older children to play with younger ones, rather as paired reading operates.

ADD AND TAKE

KEY AREA
Addition and
subtraction

RESOURCES
Pack of playing
cards
Whiteboards and
pens (optional)

GROUP SIZE
Partners, larger
groups or whole
class

○ Remove the court cards from a pack of playing cards
  and shuffle the remaining cards.

○ Divide the pack into two reasonably equal piles, face
  down, and explain that as soon as the top two cards
  are turned the numbers shown must be added and,
  also, the difference between them calculated as
  quickly as possible. Practise a few turns to
  demonstrate.

○ Answers can be recorded on paper or a whiteboard
  and solutions then revealed after each one, or after a
  series if used as a quiz.

○ This also works well in a group as a friendly knock-
  out game where the answers are called as soon as they
  are calculated. Once a child has answered, she/he
  must not call another answer until everyone else has
  achieved one. In the interests of maintaining self-
  esteem, keep the pressure to a minimum and always
  include a second, third or fourth round where
  individual members can challenge themselves to
  improve their own response time.

DIFFERENTIATION

○ Younger or lower ability children could concentrate
  on either just adding or just taking away; the higher
  value cards should be removed along with the court
  cards.

○ Use multiplication and division of the numbers
  instead of addition and subtraction, remembering that
  some pairs of numbers will have remainders when
  divided.

○ Use all four rules together.

○ Try an add/take variation where the two numbers are
  first added together and then subtracted from 20. In
  this case the only number required to be called or
  recorded is the final solution.

KEY AREA	RESOURCES	GROUP SIZE
Odd and even numbers	Blank cards Stopwatch or timer	Pairs

○ Write a range of numbers – some odd, some even – on about 30 blank cards and shuffle the cards.
○ Partner A times partner B as she/he sorts the cards into separate piles of even and odd numbers.
○ Once the piles are checked, the cards are shuffled and the partners swap roles.
○ See who wins after two or three turns each.

DIFFERENTIATION

○ For younger children, spots arranged in groups of two or three can be used on fewer cards.
○ The numbers can be chosen depending on the age and ability of the pairs, i.e. single digit to six digits and decimal numbers. Remember to use tricky numbers, such as 33,332 or 44.3, and use 0 on the end of some even numbers., e.g. 530, 53.0.

ODD AND EVEN

MATCHING PAIRS

KEY AREA	RESOURCES	GROUP SIZE
Four rules	Blank number cards	2–4

○ Make a set of about 15 pairs of cards by writing matching pairs on them, e.g. 16 and 2 × 8 or 50 and 25 + 25. The matching questions and answers will depend on the ability of the players and the function to be stressed.

○ Shuffle the cards and lay them out face down in uniform rows. The players then take turns to try to turn over two matching cards.

○ If unsuccessful, the pair of cards is turned back in the original positions, with each player trying to memorize where previously revealed cards are.

○ If successful, the player keeps the matching pair and has a further go.

○ When all cards are matched the players count their cards to see who has won.

FURTHER THEMES FOR THE SAME GAME

○ Fractions – make a set of cards with equivalent fractions to match, extending to decimal fractions and percentages.

○ Vocabulary – make a set of matches with the signs paired with the associated words, e.g. + and total. Older children can use the full range of signs to include: <, >, (n, n), ≈, ^{2}, √.

○ Measures – use equivalent measurements of varying units, e.g. 1½ metres and 1 metre 50cm or 3.4kg and 3kg 400g.

○ Shape – matching cards have drawn 2D and/or 3D shapes paired with their names.

VARIATION
All cards are revealed at the start and players are timed in turn to match them.

DIFFERENTIATION
The chances of turning over a successful pair are increased if more than one way of matching is used, e.g. 30 and 2 × 15 as well as 30 and 38 – 8.

KEY AREA	RESOURCES	GROUP SIZE
Four rules/probability	Two dice per pair Pencils and paper	Pairs

○ Set up a 3 × 3 noughts and crosses grid. Place a number in each box, choosing from 0–12 if not including multiplication, 0–36 if multiplying is allowed. Chosen numbers can be repeated if wished.

○ Partners decide who is to be O and who is X and then take turns to throw the dice. If the spots thrown calculate to a number written on the grid (see Differentiation below) the appropriate O or X is entered over it. A row of noughts or crosses wins the game.

○ Players take turns to start in subsequent games and keep a record of wins.

○ Discuss the probability of certain numbers coming up, e.g. 0 will result from a subtraction for any double and, if adding, there are more ways of making 6, 7 or 8 with two dice than of making 2–5 or 9–12.

DIFFERENTIATION

○ If dice are to be added only, the numbers in the grid will have to be between 2 and 12 inclusive.

○ For add and take possibilities, use 0–12, remembering there is only one way to make 11 and 12.

○ For all four rules use 0–12 plus 15, 16, 18, 20, 24, 25, 30 and 36, remembering again that the higher numbers have fewer chances of turning up.

○ For tables practice, this game can be used with multiplication only. In this case the numbers possible to use would be: 1–6 plus 8, 9, 10, 12, 15, 16, 18, 20, 24, 25, 30 and 36.

NOUGHTS AND CROSSES 1: FOUR RULES

IDEA 5

KEY AREA	RESOURCES	GROUP SIZE
Times tables	A4 lined file paper	Any
	Card	
	Stopwatch or timer	

TABLES 1: SPEED

○ Children write, large and clearly on every third line of a sheet of lined file paper, a chosen times table, leaving out the final answer, thus:

$0 \times 3 =$

$1 \times 3 =$

$2 \times 3 =$

to $10 \times 3 =$ or to 12×3 if the children are accustomed to that.

○ Cut small squares of card which will fit comfortably at the end of each number sentence and the children then write the answers to the table on the card squares.

○ Lay out the prepared card squares randomly, either face up or face down depending on the degree of difficulty sought.

○ Set a timer and get the children to place the card answer squares in the correct places as quickly as possible.

○ Subsequent turns can be used for the children to beat their own times.

EXTENSION

○ Prepare the tables sheet in a random order, i.e.

$4 \times 3 =$

$8 \times 3 =$

$6 \times 3 =$ (and so on)

○ Practise the inverse of any table by preparing the sheet with the answers and make the cards 1–10 (or 1–12). It would be advisable in this case to write the number sentences in random order to avoid the child simply placing the numbers in order.

$18 \div 3 =$

$12 \div 3 =$

$24 \div 3 =$ and so on.

○ Try the 15s, 25s, or any others for those who enjoy a challenge.

DIFFERENTIATION

Choose appropriate tables to work with depending on age, ability or class focus.

KEY AREA   RESOURCES   GROUP SIZE
Number   PE mats   Whole class or
                                          large group

This game is ideally played at the end of a floor work PE
lesson as part of the clearing away process.

o Spread PE mats around the floor with just enough
   space between them for the children to jump from
   one to another.
o Have the children island hop from one mat to
   another, no stopping allowed.
o Explain that you will call a number (the simplest
   version) or a sum and that number or answer must be
   made up by the corresponding amount of children
   sitting on each island (mat). Any islands with the
   wrong number – either too few or too many – are out.
o Any children who are out can put away the outer
   mats as they go, ensuring that there are enough mats
   left for the rest of the players to use.

DIFFERENTIATION
Vary the degree of difficulty with the numbers or
questions called.

o The basic game is to call the actual number. The
   more advanced version asks the children to calculate
   simple sums using all four rules.
o For the more able, try division and subtraction using
   higher numbers, 2 squared, 3 squared, square roots
   and the first five prime numbers.

KEY AREA
Number

RESOURCES
0–9 number
cards

GROUP SIZE
Individually or
in pairs within
groups or whole
class

IDEA

7

○ Shuffle a set of 0–9 cards and place them face down.
○ Decide how many cards are to be turned – two will
  be the easiest.
○ The player must place the cards in order to make: the
  largest and smallest possible numbers; the largest and
  smallest even numbers; and the largest and smallest
  odd numbers. If played in pairs, the partner helps or
  checks.
○ If only two cards are to be used, do not include 0 and
  either ensure that there is one odd and one even or,
  better still, do not call for an odd or even category.
○ If three or more cards are used and all even or all odd
  cards turn up, swap a card.

DIFFERENTIATION
Adjust the number of cards to suit age and ability. This
activity can also be used for decimal numbers. Make one
extra card with a decimal point.

LARGEST AND SMALLEST

CIRCLE TIME

KEY AREA	RESOURCES	GROUP SIZE
Number	None	Any number of children in groups of about 8–12

The object of this game is to score points by being the first to complete a circuit of the group circle.

○ Have the groups sitting in large, equal-sized circles.
○ Allocate a number to each child in the group. The numbers should correspond to answers to sums which will be called out. They do not have to be consecutive but this is advisable until everyone becomes accustomed to the game.
○ Jot down the numbers allocated so that you can keep track of the calls, giving everyone a turn.
○ Let us say, for example, you have allocated the numbers 1–10. Call 'How many 3s in 15?' Child number 5 from each group should immediately jump up and run right round the outside of the circle and sit back down in their original place.
○ The first child to sit back down scores a point for that group.
○ Continue calling sums for the rest of the numbers. When all the numbers have had a turn, tot up the points to find the overall winning group.

DIFFERENTIATION

There is no limit to the possibilities for complex questioning. If you make a list of questions, say, on the tables you are learning, or equal/decimal fractions, simply allocate the answers at random around the group.

With very small children, use a large foam dice in the centre of a group of six. Children count the spots to cue their circle run. In this case, decide the number of dice throws to determine the end of the game as some numbers will, of course, arise more than once.

KEY AREA	RESOURCES	GROUP SIZE	**IDEA**
Four rules	Blank number cards	Small groups or whole class	**9**
	Scrap paper for jottings		

FIRST TO THE FACT

This is aimed at upper KS2 children. Reduce the number range for younger or less able children.

○ Distribute blank number cards to the children in the group or class, giving smaller groups three or four cards each, a whole class about two per child. These cards can be handmade or the wipe-clean variety. They can, of course, be reused any number of times for this or any other activity.

○ Have the children write large, clear numbers between 2 and 50 on the cards. Try to obtain numbers throughout the range, but it does not matter if some are repeated.

○ The cards are placed face down on the table with no one knowing where any particular number is.

○ Make a card for each of the four function signs.

○ Choose a child to turn over a card, let's say it was 14, and another child to turn a second, say 26.

○ Somebody else picks out one of the function signs, again at random. If it is the × sign then the sum formed is 14×26.

○ The first person to provide the correct answer is the winner.

○ You can make any rules to determine winners, such as a running total to produce an overall winner after a given number of sums or amount of time.

○ Clearly, some of the sums produced can be very easy and some quite difficult. It is worth having a calculator handy to double check answers before they are produced by the first child.

DIFFERENTIATION

You can make the calculations easier or harder by varying the numbers written on the cards or removing the multiplication and/or division signs. Include decimal numbers for a further challenge.

ROUND THE WORLD

KEY AREA
Four rules

RESOURCES
None

GROUP SIZE
Any

This game is an old favourite. It can be used to reinforce any aspect being covered at the time, from times tables to decimals, fractions and percentages. The object of the game is to be the first of a pair to call out the correct answer to a question. For this example tables are used as the theme.

o Choose a child to start who stands behind a seated 'challenger'.

o Ask a question of the pair, say, 5 × 4 .

o The rest of the group or class must remain silent but the first of the chosen pair to call out the correct answer wins. If a wrong answer is given, second tries should not be allowed and the other child of the pair has an opportunity to calculate with less pressure. If both give a wrong answer, none at all or both call at the same time then a new question should be given until a clear winner results.

o The winner moves to the next seated child (or 'country') and a new challenge begins. If the winner is the seated child then the seat is taken by the loser as the journey continues around the group or class.

o The overall winner is the child who has moved successfully around most 'countries'. To give every traveller a fair chance, once everyone in the group or class has had a challenge, keep going until the last traveller loses a question.

DIFFERENTIATION
Vary the questions asked to suit age and ability.

This activity develops the ability to make rapid mental calculations and select 'best use' from the results. The children will become familiar with the rules very quickly after the first game but it does require careful explanation initially.

○ With everyone together, give examples of how a throw of two dice can be calculated during the game, e.g. 4 and 2 can be: $4 + 2 = 6$; $4 - 2 = 2$; $4 \times 2 = 8$; $4 \div 2 = 2$; or 5 and 5 can be: $5 + 5 = 10$; $5 - 5 = 0$; $5 \times 5 = 25$; $5 \div 5 = 1$. Not all throws can be used for division.

○ The game is played in pairs. To help maintain flow, it is best for player A to complete all throws before passing over to player B.

○ The partner who reaches 50 in the fewest throws of the dice wins.

○ Throw the dice and calculate possible answers, beginning with adding or multiplication to take the score towards the 50. Record the running total on paper.

○ The 6 has a special role in altering the direction of play: once the first throw is out of the way, a 6 on *one or both* dice alters the function from add to take or take to add, so if you are adding and reached, say, 23, and the next throw is, say, 4 and 6, the result chosen by calculating the spots, must be subtracted. In this case it would be best to choose the smallest possible number, i.e. $6 - 4 = 2$. The results of further throws must be subtracted until another 6 is thrown, when results must be added again and so on.

○ If at any point subtractions reach 0 or beyond, make the decision either to continue with subtractions into negative numbers or stay at zero until a 6 is thrown, remembering to record the number of throws used.

○ Players can go as far above the target number as the dice take them.

MAKE 50!

- When a zero calculation is used, i.e. when a double is used as a subtraction, the throw must still be counted towards the final number of throws.
- Most 50s are reached in about 10–12 throws but an agreement could be made for a player to pass the dice over to a partner if the 50 has not been reached by the twentieth throw (or another agreed number).
- If the second player exceeds the first player's number of throws, she/he should be allowed to continue and make the target.
- Play the best of three games if time permits.

DIFFERENTIATION

- To simplify the game, thry any combination of: a) use only adding and subtracting; b) remove the 6 rule; c) reduce the 50 target number; d) count the number of throws to pass the target number rather than reach it exactly.
- To make the game much harder, use three dice with a target of 100 or 150. This gives more complex possibilities for using mixed operations in any one throw.

Multi-step
questions and
inverse
operations

Blank number
cards
Pencils and paper
Calculators

Pairs or small
groups

This develops the concept of multi-step operations.

○ Use about 20 blank cards per group, and write a
   number on each within a chosen range to suit the
   ability of the players.
○ On each of another 20 cards write the function
   symbol: +, −, ×, ÷. Have six cards of each symbol but
   only two cards for ÷.
○ Shuffle the number cards and place them in a pile
   face down. Do the same with the symbol cards.
○ Children can take turns to work through a sum or
   cooperate on the calculations. They must record the
   sum in all its stages as they go. The number of steps
   should be decided at the outset.
○ Turn the top number card, let's say it is 23, then a
   symbol card, say +, and a second number, perhaps 9.
   The calculation is then made, i.e. 23 + 9 = 32.
○ This answer is then used as the first part of the next
   step, made by drawing another symbol card followed
   by another number. For this example: the 32 with ×
   and 15. This would produce 480. The 480 would then
   be used for a further step if desired.
○ If the division symbol is revealed and the numbers
   picked are not divisible, another function is chosen.
   The division is calculated as soon as two numbers
   appear which *are* divisible.
○ The calculator can be used either for simple
   calculator practice or to check paper-and-pencil
   calculations.
○ When the final calculation is made, set the challenge
   to 'undo' the whole process by inverse operations and
   return to the first card chosen.

DIFFERENTIATION

○ Simplify the calculations by any combination of: a)
   restrict the range of numbers on the cards; b) restrict

STEP BY STEP

the functions to simply adding or adding and subtracting; c) limit the number of steps to two.

o If anyone enjoys a challenge, include some decimal numbers or include extra division symbol cards to result in decimal answers to be carried forward.

KEY AREA
Positive and
negative
numbers

RESOURCES
Blank number
cards
Whiteboards and
pens

GROUP SIZE
Best in small
groups but it can
work with the
full class

IDEA

13

This game is for upper KS2 or those familiar with the
concept of positive and negative numbers. Make two sets
of number cards. Set one is numbered –1 to –9, each of
the nine to be written twice, giving 18 cards in all. Set
two has nine cards numbered –1 to –9 and another nine
cards numbered 1 to 9, giving nine positive and nine
negative numbers. These will be necessary to allow the
possibility of adding either a positive or a negative
number to a negative number.

- Shuffle both sets of cards and place them face down
  in separate piles.
- Turn the top card of Set one, let's say it is –2.
- Explain that the top card of Set two must be added to
  this number and turn that card – let's say that it is –5.
- The children write the answer on their whiteboards,
  in this case –7.
- Repeat the card-turning at whatever speed is
  appropriate for the group and include any competitive
  element you wish.

LET'S BE POSITIVE . . . OR NEGATIVE

KEY AREA
Times tables

RESOURCES
Paper and pencils
Counters
(optional)

GROUP SIZE
Any

o Choose one of the tables, say the fours.

o The children draw a 3 × 3 grid and in each box write their own choices of a mixture of any of the multiples, i.e. in this example 0, 4, 8, 12, and so on, and the times number, i.e. any from 0–10 or 12.

o When everyone has a completed grid, call random questions in the four times table – both forwards and inverse – giving an appropriate time for calculation and remembering to keep a record of the questions called.

o The players use counters to cover squares which correspond to the answers or, alternatively, score through with a single line so as not to obscure the number entered.

o In true Bingo style, the player who first fills her/his card calls out, and the numbers are checked to ensure against mistakes.

VARIATION
With slightly larger squares on the 3 × 3 grid, the players write the questions in the boxes, e.g. 3 × 4, 8 × 4, 40 ÷ 4, and so on. The caller calls random multiples and dividends.

NB – Whichever way the game is played there will be some numbers which can be used either as a multiple or a dividend; in this example, 0, 4, 8 and 12. This is only significant in the lower order tables and can be overcome, if thought necessary, by ruling that only one or two of such numbers are permissible.

DIFFERENTIATION
Vary the times table chosen.

KEY AREA	RESOURCES	GROUP SIZE
Probability	Pack of cards	Pairs

○ Shuffle the cards.
○ The players take turns to hold the cards and reveal one at a time.
○ Player A turns the top card and player B decides whether the next will be higher or lower, given that 7 is in the middle, the ace is low and jack, queen, king ascend in that order.
○ If player B is correct she/he keeps the two cards. If the guess is incorrect, the cards go to the 'dealer', player A. If the cards are the same value they are not counted by either player.
○ The game continues in this way until all the cards are used.
○ Both players count and record the number of cards they win.
○ The cards are then shuffled and the players swap roles.
○ The overall winner is the player with the highest combined total over the two games.

VARIATION
Include the possibility of guessing that the pair of cards drawn will be the same. If this is the rule then the dealer keeps any such pair if a guess of simply 'higher' or 'lower' is given. If a player guesses correctly that any two cards are the same, however, she/he keeps them and, in addition, captures four further cards from her/his opponent.

DIFFERENTIATION
Remove the court cards and the tens for an easier version.

HIGHER OR LOWER

KEY AREA
Four rules

RESOURCES
Pencils and paper
or whiteboards,
Calculators
(optional)

GROUP SIZE
Any

This is just the same as the spelling game but with numbers.

○ A child calculates a secret number sentence and draws boxes in place of digits, leaving gaps wherever a function sign should be. The equals sign is put in at the start as that would be an obvious call for the guessers. Thus 23 + 94 = 117 would be written:

☐☐ ☐ ☐☐ = ☐☐☐

○ Everyone else guesses numbers or signs which might be in the equation. Wrong guesses are recorded as reminders, and a part of the traditional gallows is drawn. Correct guesses are written into the equation wherever they occur.

○ The object is, of course, to encourage logical thought rather than random guesses.

○ The first to guess the whole equation correctly sets the next puzzle.

DIFFERENTIATION

○ Adjust the possibilities to the age and ability of the group. Naturally, the simplest would be to use single-digit numbers and only addition.

○ There is no limit at the upper ability level, especially if calculators are used. Decimal points can be included (in a box). Use more than one function, possibly on both sides of the equation and incorporate the use of BODMAS (the order of calculation, being Brackets Off – Division – Multiplication – Addition – Subtraction).

IDEA

17

GIVE ME THE FRACTION

○ Make appropriate fraction cards for the number of
   Multilink cubes used, say 12. In this example, the
   fraction cards would be: any number of twelfths,
   sixths, quarters, thirds, halves. Any means of making
   one whole, e.g. %, can also be included.
○ Place the [12] cubes in a fixed line.
○ Shuffle the fraction cards and place them face down.
○ Players take turns to turn a card and take the correct
   number of cubes for that fraction, e.g. the ¾ card
   should render nine cubes separated.

DIFFERENTIATION
○ The simplest way to play is using varying numbers of
   bricks and the child finds just half or quarter.
○ Use the single numerator for intermediate difficulty.
○ For the ultimate challenge, include decimal fractions
   and percentages with larger multiples of cubes.

SEQUENTIAL PATTERNS

KEY AREA
Sequences

RESOURCES
Assorted
coloured cubes
Photocopied
grids (see
preparation
below)
Colouring
pencils

GROUP SIZE
Any

This is an early sequencing activity for KS1.

○ Draw a line of 12 blank squares, either adjoining in a straight line or curved like a snake. The squares should match the size of cubes to be used. Photocopy for current and future use.

○ Explain the nature of sequential, repeating patterns.

○ The children make a row of 12 coloured cubes in a sequential pattern using a specified number of different colours, say, three.

○ The pattern produced must then be recorded exactly onto the photocopied sheet.

○ Keep the resources available for use in a range of choosing activities.

DIFFERENTIATION

○ Vary the number of colours used, keeping to factors of 12.

○ Extend the line to 18 squares.

KEY AREA
Number

RESOURCES
None

GROUP SIZE
Any

IDEA

19

The object of this game is to identify a secret number within ten questions.

○ A chosen person thinks of a number. This can be restricted to a two-digit number or have no restrictions placed on it at all. Decimal numbers, however, can be somewhat frustrating unless there are limits placed on the overall number of digits.

○ Guessers ask questions to which the only answers can be either 'Yes' or 'No'. Wild guesses should be discouraged in favour of questions which seek logical information and continually narrow down the possibilities.

○ Typical questions would be: 'Is it odd or even?', 'Is it a three-digit number?', 'Is it divisible by 5?', 'Is it below 50?'

DIFFERENTIATION

Vary the size of the numbers used.

WHAT'S MY NUMBER?

KEY AREA
Times tables

RESOURCES
None

GROUP SIZE
5–6 to whole
class

The object of this game is simply to count consecutively from one to however many you would like to reach. The difference is using words instead of certain numbers, so:

o If the number is divisible by 2 then 'buzz' should be said.
o If the number is divisible by 3 then 'fizz' should be called.
o If the number is divisible by both 2 and 3 then 'buzz fizz' is the response.

The first 12 numbers would therefore sound, 'one, buzz, fizz, buzz, five, buzz fizz, seven, buzz, fizz, buzz, eleven, buzz fizz'.

o Each member of the group gives the next number, or alternative expression, either in regular turn or randomly around the room or group. If an incorrect response is given, the next person must attempt it rather than have it corrected. A class of 30 children new to this game, therefore, may only reach about 18 (buzz fizz) by the time they have all had a go, but regular playing improves their ability very quickly.
o A decision can be made, depending on the character and experience of the group, whether or not to impose penalties for incorrect responses. A typical set of penalties is to stand after a first fault, hold an ear on the second, hold the nose on the third, and so on. These forfeits are removed by subsequent correct responses.

DIFFERENTIATION

o Begin with just 'buzz' for even numbers.
o Insert 'fizz' for the threes when the three times table is more familiar.
o Introduce 'plop' for fives once the game is familiar.
o For a real challenge use an additional 'hooray' for square numbers and 'eek' for prime numbers.

IDEA

21

This is based on the crazy sentence game.

○ Explain that things will be written at the top of the strip of paper in a particular order and passed on round the group. Each time something is written the paper has to be folded back so that it is not seen by the next person. The folds always have to be just once backwards and the new number or symbol must be written against the fold, at the top.

○ Each member of the group has a strip of paper and secretly writes a two-digit number at the top.

○ She/he folds the paper to the back, concealing only the number and passes it to the group member to her/his left.

○ Each group member then draws a function sign, +, − , ×, or ÷, at the top of the new strip of paper where it has been folded. This is then folded over again and passed to the left.

○ The third person writes a single-digit number at the top, folds it in the same way and passes it on.

○ If there are five people in the group, the fourth player adds a function sign and the fifth a two-digit number.

○ For a group of seven, the sixth player adds a sign and the seventh a single-digit number.

○ When everyone in the group has written something on every piece of paper then it is time to begin the calculations. Whatever strip each member ends up with, that is the one she/he must work out.

○ Decide whether the rules of BODMAS (see Idea 16) should be followed or calculations made in the order of writing – or perhaps both. Also make a decision on the use of calculators.

○ Allow individuals to help each other work out the problems.

MATHS CONSEQUENCES

DIFFERENTIATION

o Beginners work in groups of three and use only addition and subtraction.

o To avoid possible negative number results allow the minus sign only as the first function, i.e. the initial two-digit number minus the single digit.

o To avoid decimals or fractions do not include division.

o To ensure decimals or fractions insist on division.

o Include the possibility of decimal numbers but only to one decimal place.

IDEA

22

KEY AREA	RESOURCES	GROUP SIZE
Decimals	2cm squared paper	Any
	Scissors	

This is an easy-to-make aid for multiplication and division by 10, 100 and 1,000.

○ Each child will require up to ten strips of 2cm squared paper, each about 20cm long by 2cm wide and put aside.

○ Cut one strip the same length but 6cm wide.

○ Fold the 6cm-wide strip in half, lengthwise. This should produce a crease through the middle row of squares.

○ Find the middle square of the folded row.

○ Carefully cut two slits, a little less than 1cm apart, from the folded edge into the middle square, cutting to the printed horizontal lines. This will give a bar just under 1cm wide and 2cm long in the middle of the strip.

○ Open out the 6cm strip and mark a decimal point clearly on the bar.

○ For demonstration purposes, have the children write a number, say '360,000', on one of the 2cm strips. They must begin the number in the first square at the left and ensure that each digit is written centrally in its own square, allowing at least 1cm between digits.

○ Thread this strip through the slits under the bar so that it can be slid to and fro giving different values depending on where the number is divided by the decimal point.

○ Give a few examples, such as, 'Make the number read 360', pointing out that any number of zeros can be included on the end after the decimal point. 'Divide this by 10', which means move the digits one place to the right. If the children do this correctly they will see clearly that they end up with 36 or 36.0000. 'Multiply this 36 by 100', which means moving the digits two places to the left. The children should see that the answer is 3,600.00.

o When the children are confident with the process, set
   questions which they can check by using the blank
   strip.

TIP
Pre-write strings of digits for multiplication and division
exercises and photocopy. Cut these into strips as
necessary.

KEY AREA	RESOURCES	GROUP SIZE
Prime numbers	Three dice	Any
	One timer per group	

This is a game for older and more able children who are familiar with at least the lower range of prime numbers. Tell the children that any throw of three dice can result in a prime number, when any of the four rules are applied. Give a few examples to show how this works, i.e. a throw of 2, 4 and 5 could be simply $2 + 4 + 5 = 11$. A throw of 1, 4 and 5, however, is more tricky but it can be done either with $5 - (4 - 1) = 2$ or $(5 - 4) + 1 = 2$.

There are a number of ways to play the game:

Option 1
o Players take turns to throw the dice and calculate their own throw.
o A minute timer is set as soon as the dice are thrown.
o Each player scores points equal to the prime number correctly calculated. The higher value prime numbers are less easily achieved.
o If an answer is not reached within the time limit or is incorrect then no points are scored.

Option 2
o Players take turns to throw the dice but all then, individually, calculate a prime number. The timing and scoring is the same as option 1.

Option 3 (Better played simply for the satisfaction of obtaining correct answers rather than in competition)
o Play as a class with nominated child/ren throwing the dice.
o Time the calculations as before, with the children completing them on whiteboards.

VARIATION
Try the same game but find square – or cube – numbers.

IN YOUR PRIME

IDEA 24

KEY AREA	RESOURCES	GROUP SIZE
Four rules	Three dice One timer per group	Any

Demonstrate how a throw of three dice can be multiplied and/or added to produce the highest possible number, e.g. a throw of 2, 4 and 5 could be multiplied together in any order to make 40. It becomes much more interesting, however, when a 1 is included in the throw. If the numbers are simply multiplied together then it will not produce the highest possible score. Using the example of a 1, 4, 5 throw, these are the possibilities:

$1 \times 4 \times 5 = 20$

$(1 + 5) \times 4 = 24$

$(1 + 4) \times 5 = 25$

The trick is adding the 1 to the smaller of the other two and multiplying by the larger.

There are a number of ways to play the game:

Option 1
○ Players take turns to throw the dice and calculate their own throw.
○ A minute timer is set as soon as the dice are thrown.
○ Each player scores points equal to the number correctly calculated.
○ If an answer is not reached within the time limit or is incorrect then no points are scored.

Option 2
○ Players take turns to throw the dice but all then, individually, calculate the highest possible number.
○ The timing and scoring is the same as option 1.

Option 3 (Better played simply for the satisfaction of obtaining correct answers rather than in competition)
○ Play as a class with nominated child/ren throwing the dice.
○ Time the calculations as before, with children completing them on whiteboards.

VARIATION

Play the same game but the object is to find the smallest possible number, using any of the four rules. It can be used to reinforce negative numbers, e.g. $1 - 4 - 5 = -8$ but it is perhaps more challenging to make the object to achieve 0 or to get as near as possible to it. In this example 0 can be reached with $5 - 4 - 1$. Using the example of a 6, 3, 2 throw and the range of four rules, this could be: $6 - (3 \times 2) = 0$ or $6 \div 3 - 2 = 0$. The winners, if scores are kept, would be those with the lowest number of points.

DIFFERENTIATION

For easier versions:

○ use just two dice
○ play using simple addition and subtraction.

DOUBLES AND QUADS

KEY AREA	RESOURCES	GROUP SIZE
Multiplication	Whiteboards (optional)	Any

Try these quick-fire, real-life questions for consolidating doubling and times 4 (double and double again). You may wish to prepare a set of questions but it is quite easy to be spontaneous.

Remind the children that a short-cut to multiplication by 4 is double and double again. Ask a number of questions requiring doubling or quadrupling to find the answer, e.g. 'How many arms on 12 people?', 'How many legs on nine cows?'

Suggestions for doubles:

○ Wings on penguins (or other birds), aeroplanes
○ Eyes on people, snakes, birds, horses
○ Ears on rabbits, giants
○ Hands/feet on people
○ Handles on doors
○ Goalposts on football pitches.

Suggestions for quadruples:

○ Legs on elephants (or other four-legged animals), chairs, tables
○ Wheels on cars
○ Prongs on forks
○ Corners/sides on squares/rectangles/parallelograms.

There are a number of ways to operate this activity, such as:

○ Using whiteboards showing answers on the given signal
○ As a mental arithmetic 'test'
○ As a warm-up lesson starter
○ To decide an order of leaving, i.e. form a line for leaving at the end of a session in the order of who answers correctly.

DIFFERENTIATION
Vary the numbers to be doubled and quadrupled according to ability.

KEY AREA
Fractions

RESOURCES
Dominoes (not
necessarily a set)
Calculators
Paper and pencils

GROUP SIZE
Pairs or small
groups

IDEA

26

FRACTION DOMINOES

This is a game for upper KS2. Some domino sets include pieces with up to nine spots and these will extend the range of possibilities in this game.

○ Remove any dominoes which include a blank and spread out the rest, face down.
○ Players take turns to turn over a domino and place it so that the fewest number of spots is above the largest, rather as a fraction but with spots in the positions of denominator and numerator.
○ The drawn common fraction must be converted to a decimal fraction and then to a percentage, thus ⅖ becomes 0.4 (2 ÷ 5 on the calculator) and 40%. The player records the decimal fraction as a score to be added to all the others made. It follows that any double will be the value of 1 or 100%. For the purposes of this game ⅓ can be 0.33 or 33% and ⅔ can be 0.67 or 67%.
○ Players score a bonus point if they successfully simplify any drawn equation, e.g. ⅙ to ⅔.
○ Once turned, each domino must be removed from play. When all the dominoes have been used – with an equal number of turns per player – everyone totals their scores and the highest number wins.
○ Players can help each other with any of the calculations as high scores are a matter of luck.

VARIATION

Try playing the game with vulgar fractions.

○ The revealed domino is interpreted with the higher number of spots as the numerator.
○ There will be no simplification bonuses.
○ Any double will be worth only one point whereas all other combinations of spots are worth more than one, so ⁶⁄₁ will have a value of 6.
○ Decide whether or not to include percentages with this version.

KEY AREA	RESOURCES	GROUP SIZE
Number	0–9 number cards	Any

The object of this game is to say the name of a number from a given number of digits.

○ Use two sets of 0–9 number cards.
○ Shuffle the cards and place them in a pile face down.
○ Agree a number of cards to be turned, say, five. This can change during the game if appropriate.
○ The cards are turned, say, 7, 3, 0, 2, 7 and the player names the number, 'seventy-three thousand and twenty-seven'. Discard a zero if it turns up first, or make it the second digit.
○ Success can be purely for personal satisfaction or a scoring system can be easily devised if players are in pairs and are well matched.

DIFFERENTIATION

○ Adjust to age and ability the number of cards turned in any go.
○ For an added element of difficulty, include a number of decimal point cards, treating them as an extra when they turn up – in the example above of a five-digit number, six cards would be turned if one was a decimal point. Discard any further decimal point cards if one is already turned.

IDEA 28

REMEMBER ME

Simply, a challenge to find the longest number the children can remember.

○ Use several sets of 0–9 number cards.
○ Shuffle the cards and place them in a pile face down.
○ Challenge the player(s) to remember, say, a six-digit number.
○ The player(s) must not write anything down but must remember the number as it is revealed one digit at a time.
○ Turn [6] cards, one by one and allowing enough time for each to be fixed in the mind. Discard a zero if it turns up first.
○ When all [6] are revealed, allow a further few seconds and turn them face down again in the order they were presented.
○ Now the player(s) must recall the number. Decide whether to wait for the full number to be given before revealing the cards again to check or to reveal one card at a time as the digits are recalled.
○ Success can be purely for personal satisfaction or a scoring system can be easily devised. It is also fun for pairs to challenge each other, increasing the number of digits each turn, on a 'sudden death' rule.

DIFFERENTIATION

For an added element of difficulty, include a number of decimal point cards, treating them as an extra when they turn up – in the example above of a six-digit number, seven cards would be turned if one was a decimal point. Discard any further decimal point cards if one is already turned.

HOW MANY WAYS?

KEY AREA	RESOURCES	GROUP SIZE
Number	Paper and pencils	Teams of 2–5

Try this team quiz for KS2.

○ Set up the teams with one member nominated to write down the answers.

○ Explain that they should confer but without allowing other teams to overhear.

○ The same question goes to all teams each time and will take the form of a number.

○ Once given the number, say 2, the team must write down as many 'two' words or 'two' associations as they can in a given amount of time. The length of time will vary depending on how many words are likely to be derived from any given number.

○ Examples of what a team might have for 2 are: double, twice, duet, duo, bicycle, biplane, binoculars, bicentenary, pair, scissors, trousers, shoes, spectacles, fortnight, weekend. Accept any reasonably logical link with the given number.

○ Team points are scored for each acceptable answer.

○ Other numbers particularly suitable for this game, with examples of responses are:

> 1 – solo, single, first, monorail, unicycle, annual
>
> 3 – trio, third, treble, triple, triangle, triplets
>
> 4 – quads, any four-sided 2D shape, tetrahedron, quadruped (or any four-legged animal)
>
> 5 – pentagon, The Pentagon, fingers of hand, toes of foot, fifth, pentathlon, Guy Fawkes
>
> 6 – sixth, hexagon, half-a-dozen, honeycomb, dice, cube
>
> 7 – seventh, 20p piece, 50p piece, heptagon, week, September
>
> 8 – eighth, octagon, octogenarian, October, Hanukkah, spider
>
> 10 – decimal, tenth, December, decagon, two hands, two feet, decade, decathlon
>
> 12 – twelfth, dodecagon, Twelfth Night, dozen, year

○ Bonus points could be awarded for the first team to come up with the number associated with a word called, e.g. score (20); century (100); gross (144); weeks in a year/cards in a pack (52); football team (11), cat's lives (9), dalmatians (101), millennium (1,000).

DIFFERENTIATION
Ensure that teams are evenly balanced for ability.

KEY AREA
Venn diagrams

RESOURCES
Blank number
cards
Small PE hoops

GROUP SIZE
2–4

SORTED FOR NUMBER

Make a set of number cards appropriate to the age and ability of the group and the area of number on which you want to focus. This example uses even numbers and multiples of 5.

○ Make number cards as follows:
  – four multiples of 5, ending in 5
  – two multiples of 5 ending in 0
  – three even numbers not ending in 0
  – two odd numbers not ending in 5.
○ Spread the prepared number cards randomly.
○ Overlap two small PE hoops, one labelled 'even numbers' and the other labelled 'multiples of 5'.
○ Set the task to sort the number cards into the correct hoops, remembering that some of the cards (those ending in 0) will need to go into the overlapped area and some (the odd numbers not ending in 5) will need to be placed outside the hoops.

DIFFERENTIATION
Vary the complexity of the categories.

KEY AREA
Four rules

RESOURCES
0–9 cards
Blank cards

GROUP SIZE
2–4 of similar
ability

GET THE WORD

This game introduces a mildly competitive element into four rules vocabulary.

Make a set of word cards for the vocabulary of the four rules, i.e. plus, total, add, minus, difference between, take away, subtract, times, multiply, product, greater/more than, smaller/less than, how many . . . in . . ., share, divide.

○ The vocabulary cards are shuffled and placed in a pile, face down.
○ Turn two number cards at random.
○ When all group members are ready, the top card of the vocabulary pile is turned.
○ The first player to calculate the resulting question correctly wins and that player turns the next vocabulary card.
○ Keep going, using the same two numbers, until all the vocabulary cards have been turned.

For randomly selected numbers which do not divide exactly, decide if the winner is: the first to say 'can't' or the first to give a correct dividend, including a remainder in an acceptable form.

DIFFERENTIATION
Group similar ability children together and include only the appropriate vocabulary cards for the respective groups.

IDEA

32

KEY AREA
Number

RESOURCES
Dice
Paper and pencils
or whiteboards

GROUP SIZE
Any

FIRST TO TEN

This is a dice game which is enjoyed on many levels. The simple object is to achieve a count of 1–10 in consecutive order.

Game 1 – for the youngest players in a group with support for recording

○ At the start, make a list of the numbers 1–10 (or 1–6 if not using a second dice later).

○ Use a single dice, preferably a large foam one.

○ Players take turns to throw and the number cast is deleted from the list when it appears for the first time. Repeated numbers are ignored.

○ When the numbers 1–6 have been achieved, introduce a second dice, if appropriate, in order to count the spots for 7–10. Either discard throws of 11 and 12 or add them to the list at the start.

Game 2 – intermediate

○ At the start, make a list of the numbers 1–10.

○ Using two dice, players take turns to throw.

○ Each throw of the dice can be added, subtracted, multiplied or divided in order to make one of the numbers 1–10.

○ Numbers achieved must be deleted, reducing the possibilities as the game progresses.

○ Alternatively, it could be ruled that the numbers 1–10 must be obtained in consecutive order, which takes longer.

○ To make the game competitive, play in pairs or teams of two to find the quickest to reach all ten numbers. You will have to decide if 'quickest' refers to the fewest throws or the quickest player or team irrespective of the number of throws.

Game 3 – advanced

Same basic rules as game 2 but with a menu of modifications from which to choose:

○ Use three dice, allowing a second function in the calculations.
○ Extend the required count from 1–10 to 1–20.
○ The two functions cannot be the same in any given throw.

DIFFERENTIATION

Use the appropriate game, adapting as necessary.

NOUGHTS AND CROSSES 2: COORDINATES

KEY AREA
Coordinates

RESOURCES
Clearly visible
whiteboard or
flipchart

GROUP SIZE
Any

o Draw a 3 × 3 noughts and crosses grid on the
   whiteboard or flipchart.
o Starting from the origin 0, label the rows and
   columns 1, 2, 3.
o Choose two children as challengers – one is O and
   the other X.
o The challengers stand side by side in front of the
   grid, unable to see it and facing the rest of the group.
o Decide which player goes first, say, X.
o X gives a pair of coordinates and the cross is placed
   in that square.
o The players then take turns to give a pair of
   coordinates for their respective symbol. They have to
   visualize the grid as it fills up in order to make a line
   and to prevent their opponent doing so.
o If a player chooses a square already filled then she/he
   misses that turn.

DIFFERENTIATION
To make the game easier, label the x axis A, B, C and the
y axis 1, 2, 3. Accept only coordinates with letter first.

IDEA

34

Prepare 'families' of five cards, e.g. the 'One-der' family – 0.1, 1, 10, 100, 1,000, the 'Two-good' family, 0.2, 2, 20, 200, 2,000, the 'Three-dom' family, 0.3., 3, 30, 300, 3,000, and so on. Only six such families are needed for the game, suggestions for the others being: the 'Four-front' family, the 'Fivers' and the 'Six-cess' family.

HAPPY FAMILIES

○ Shuffle the cards and deal to the four players, starting with the player to the left of the dealer. Two players will have an extra card each but as the dealer changes in subsequent games the disadvantage will pass around the group.

○ Players look at their cards and arrange them in the families, noting which members are needed to make up the set. If a player is lucky enough to have a full family set of five then she/he puts them down.

○ The player to the left of the dealer asks the player to her/his right for a card in a family which hopefully will make a set or go towards a set. If the player asked holds that particular card she/he must pass it over and if this makes a family of five they are put down. If the requested card is not held then no other request can be made on this particular turn. Whatever the result of the request, play passes clockwise around the group.

○ Most children will simply ask for the number but players should be encouraged to ask questions such as, 'Do you have the tenths of the Three-dom family?' (0.3) or, 'Do you have the hundred of the Six-cess family?' (600).

○ Watching and listening carefully, players will learn something about the cards other players are holding and use this to their advantage.

○ The winner is the first to put down two families or the first to lose all of her/his cards.

DIFFERENTIATION
An easier game can be played using families of three, e.g. 5, 50, 500.

IDEA 35

CRACK THE CODE

KS2 children pick this up quickly and enjoy making their own code puzzles.

The object of this puzzle is to place the numbers 1–9 correctly with the letters A–J (omitting I to avoid possible confusion). All that is required to set a puzzle is careful manipulation following the key solution of [A] ? [A] = [A], so:

$A \times A = A$ (A must be 1)
$D - A = A$ (D must be 2)
$A + D = J$ (J must be 3)
$D \times J = E$ (E must be 6)
$D \times D = G$ (G must be 4)
$C \div G = D$ (C must be 8)
$J + D = F$ (F must be 5)
$C + G = H + F$ (H must be 7)
$B \div J = J$ (B must be 9)

Any letter can represent any of the numbers. It is best not to make it A = 1, B = 2, C = 3 and so on, as children tend to assume that to begin with. Once you have worked out your puzzle, which takes a few minutes, jumble up the statements and present them for solution by the group. Encourage the children to work systematically, inserting known values throughout the puzzle as they discover them.

Here is a further example for you to try:

$A + B = J$ $D - E = A$
$C \times C = C$ $E - C = C$
$F + E = A$ $E \times E = B$
$F + E = B + C$ $J - F = G$
$E \times B = H$

The nine letters do not have to be the first in the alphabet; they could comprise letters in a coded final message to be solved. Decide on the message, e.g. 'VERY WELL DONE' which has nine different letters, and use those. The corresponding numbers would be set out in order ready for the message to be deciphered.

IDEA

36

BUS STOP

This knock-out game for a lot of people is ideal as a 'party' game and also a good way to end a PE lesson. It can be played in a cleared area of the classroom but a hall is better.

○ Make up to eight bus stop signs giving simply the bus number. Choose both odd and even numbers and numbers which are multiples of tables selected for practice. The example here will be answers to the five and four times tables, using the bus numbers: 16, 25, 28, 32, 35, 36, 40, 55.

○ Place the 'bus stops' around the sides of the available space, preferably at eye level.

○ Make a set of postcards which refer to the bus numbers you have used. For this example the postcards could read: 'odd numbers'; 'even numbers'; 'even multiples of five'; 'odd multiples of five'; 'multiples of four'.

○ The group moves around in the available space until the signal is called, 'All aboard!' or similar, whereupon everyone must stand still and listen to the instructions. A card is chosen at random and read out. On picking out, say, 'odd numbers', the caller decides whether to say 'odd numbers only are running' or 'no odd numbers running today'.

○ Immediately, the players must go to an appropriate stop. Any player not at a bus stop after a given time is out. If 'odd numbers only are running' is called in this example, then buses 25, 35 and 55 should be the only numbers with a queue. Anyone waiting at the other numbers would be out.

○ A limit is placed on the number at the bus stop depending on how many players are left in the game at the time and how many different correct choices can be made.

○ As the number of players dwindles, remove buses from service until only one or two winners are left.

○ Prizes are optional.

45

DIFFERENTIATION

Choose appropriate numbers and options from the simplest level of just odd or even numbers to quite complicated three-digit requirements.

Addition and/or
multiplication

Counters
0–9 number
cards
Small PE hoops
Paper and pencils
or whiteboards
and pens
Calculators
(optional)

2–4

TIDDLYWINKS

A numerical interpretation of the traditional game, this is
best played on the floor.

o Put down a small PE hoop or similar – a marked area
   approximately 40cm across is required.
o Shuffle two or three sets of 0–9 cards and put them
   face down in the hoop/space, ensuring that they do
   not overlap and the spaces between them are very
   small.
o Players choose which colour they are to be and take
   two to five counters of that colour. The more the
   counters the more difficult the mathematics.
o The first player uses one counter to flip the others
   into the hoop, one at a time, aiming to land each on a
   card. Misses cannot be retaken.
o Any card with a counter fully on it is revealed, and
   the numbers tallied to give total points for that go.
   Numbers can be added or multiplied depending on
   the ability of the players.
o The score is recorded and the second and subsequent
   players have their turns.
o The winner is the player with the highest score.

DIFFERENTIATION
o Younger children could use a limited range of
   numbers, say, 1–4.
o For a more advanced game make cards with higher
   numbers, decimal numbers or calculations.

IDEA 38

KEY AREA
Number

RESOURCES
Counters

GROUP SIZE
4–8 players of
similar ability

WINNING COUNTERS

This is a good game for consolidating current work.

o Divide the group into two teams and allocate a
counter colour for each team. Players sit around a
table with a container in the middle to receive played
counters.
o Give each group member five counters in the team
colour.
o Ask questions covering the current mathematics work
or any previously learned concepts.
o The first to call the correct answer places one counter
in the middle.
o At the end of the game – which is as long as time
permits – total the counters in the middle for the
winning team and see who has used the most.
o The purpose of limiting the number of counters to
individuals is to remove those lucky enough to be
quicker at answering once they have reached their
quota, giving others a chance.

DIFFERENTIATION
Adjust questions according to age and ability.

KEY AREA
Number

RESOURCES
Cards in the
shape of fish
approximately
6cm long
Colouring pens
or pencils
Scissors
String
Magnets
Paper clips
Short canes

GROUP SIZE
Any

IDEA

39

GONE FISHING

The children enjoy participating in the preparation of
this game by making the fish and fishing rods. Once
made, the game can be used over and over again.

○ Cut fish shapes about 6cm long from card, allowing
  for three or four per child.
○ The children can colour one side of each to make
  them attractive but should avoid making any one fish
  very different from the others.
○ Slide a paper clip over the head end of each fish.
○ Tie a magnet to one end of a piece of string, strong
  thread or wool about 40–50cm long.
○ Tie the other end of the 'fishing line' to a short
  garden stick or 'fishing rod'.
○ Write a question on the blank side of each fish which
  corresponds to an answer written on a card left on
  dry land. These answer cards are not seen by the
  players during the game unless it is agreed that such
  clues should be given.
○ Place the fish, coloured side up, into an appropriate
  pond, which could be the floor or table top.
○ Players take turns to catch a fish, and look at the
  question on the reverse.
○ The player does the calculation – using any jottings or
  written calculations necessary – and gives the answer.
○ A non-player checks the answer cards. If the answer is
  correct, the player keeps the card, ready to be added
  to her/his final total. If the answer is wrong then no
  points are scored at all.

○ When all fish have been caught, players total up their cards to find the winner.

DIFFERENTIATION
○ Very young children can play this with spots or stars on the fish which they count.
○ Challenges at the end of KS2 could involve much larger calculations, including long multiplication, decimals, fractions, averages, and so on. Agreement would have to be reached on the use of calculators.

KEY AREA	RESOURCES	GROUP SIZE	**IDEA**
Number	Squared paper	Threes (rotating	**40**
	Colouring	with two	
	pencils	competing and	
	Mental maths	the third asking	
	questions	questions)	

PATHWAYS

This is a game to spice up mental maths. The object is to make a path from either top to bottom or side to side of a 5 × 5 grid. The pathway cannot be diagonal.

○ Draw a 5 × 5 grid on squared paper.
○ Two players choose a colour each and decide who goes first.
○ The third member of the group poses questions from published mental maths practice materials.
○ Players are asked questions in turn. If the answer is correct the player colours in any free square on the grid. If incorrect, no square is coloured. The first answer only can be taken.
○ Paths can be blocked which is, of course, part of the strategy. Players can go round a block using adjacent squares.

Note: This game can be played successfully in groups of five, i.e. two teams of two and a questionmaster.

DIFFERENTIATION
Select questions at the appropriate level.

IDEA

41

KEY AREA
Division

RESOURCES
Two or three sets
of 0–9 number
cards
Conventional
dice
Jotting paper or
whiteboards

GROUP SIZE
Any, but this
works well with
teams of 2

This game is for reluctant dividers in KS2.

○ Shuffle the cards and place them in a pile, face down.
○ The top two cards are turned to make a two-digit
  number. It can be a free choice of which card
  represents tens and which the units but, once
  decided, the order cannot be changed.
○ A dice is thrown and players must divide the two-
  digit number by the number shown as quickly as
  possible, including any remainders (see below).
○ The first correct answer scores a point.
○ Play continues until all the cards have been used.

This game works well with showing answers on
whiteboards and entrusting players with their own
scoring.

DIFFERENTIATION
○ An easier version is to ignore the cards, throw a dice
  and if it is, say, a 3, call a multiple of 3 for the
  division sum to be written on a whiteboard.
○ Decide how remainders are to be expressed. This is
  useful for consolidating rounding if calculators are
  allowed.
○ More confident players can be challenged with three-
  digit numbers.

KEY AREA
Number

RESOURCES
Computer

GROUP SIZE
Individual or
pairs

IDEA

42

Familiarize the children with calculators on computers.

o Introduce the path on your computer for setting up
   its calculator.
o Allow time to experiment with it and gain familiarity,
   e.g. provide a range of questions on the computer to
   calculate or allow the children to devise their own.
o Show some of the general functions of calculators,
   such as repeat click on = to obtain a continuous
   function result.
o Visit websites which present work suitable for
   calculator-assisted solutions.

COMPUTER CALCULATOR

IDEA

43

GET COORDINATED

KEY AREA
Coordinates

RESOURCES
Squared paper
Rulers
Pencils

GROUP SIZE
4–6

This is a fun way to consolidate coordinates in KS2. The object of this game is for players to simultaneously and covertly draw the same shape from coordinates provided independently.

o Players draw x and y axes on squared paper and number them *on the lines*, 1–10 from the origin.

o Players then take turns to give a pair of coordinates which every player must plot without the others seeing.

o Plotted points should be joined each time a new pair is given. Players should give coordinates which do not involve this path crossing itself but nothing should be said if anyone believes this to be the case.

o When every player has given a pair of coordinates, the last pair is joined to the first to complete the shape. For small groups, each player could provide two pairs of coordinates.

o Players then reveal their completed shapes which are, hopefully, identical.

VARIATION

Players take turns secretly to draw a shape and then give all of the coordinates for the other players to match.

DIFFERENTIATION

Confident players can try plotting shapes using all four quadrants.

KEY AREA
Number

RESOURCES
Large foam dice
Cards numbered
1–6 or plastic
numbers 1–6

GROUP SIZE
2–4

IDEA

44

Try this number recognition game with KS1 children.

o Each player has the numbers 1–6 in front of her/him.
o Players take turns to throw the dice.
o The first player to hold up the card with the correct
  number corresponding to the dots on the dice throw
  is the winner.

VARIATION
Roll using varying numbers of plastic cubes to be
counted as quickly as possible.

DIFFERENTIATION
o Ensure that every child has an opportunity to win.
o Use two dice with the numbers 1–12.

SPOTS AND NUMBERS

THE SIMPLE CARD GAME

KEY AREA
Addition

RESOURCES
Pack of cards
Counters

GROUP SIZE
3–6

This is an ideal introduction to card games for KS2. For this game, all picture cards count as 10 and the ace is 11. The object is to score as closely as possible to the maximum 33 by adding the value of the three cards in your hand.

o Each player has three 'lives' represented by counters shared out at the start of the game.

o Players take turns to deal three cards each, plus another set of three for the middle.

o The three middle cards are turned over.

o Players in turn, starting with the one to the left of dealer, have an opportunity to exchange one card in their hand with one in the middle. If players wish they can exchange all three cards but this reveals their hand. Any player who does not wish to make any change says 'Pass'.

o When all players have had an opportunity to change once, all cards are revealed. The player with the lowest score loses a counter. On losing the third counter, a player has one 'free ride' but is out on losing again.

o If any player is lucky enough to have three aces in their hand, all others lose a counter immediately and the round is finished.

VARIATION

o No extra cards in the middle. Instead, players take one card in turn, unseen, from the player to their left.

o A more advanced game requires only cards of the same suit to be totalled. In this case the maximum score is 31. Exchanges (one or all three cards) continue in turn until a player calls 'Stop', after which the other players have one last change if they wish. The caller must not, however, have a final change.

KEY AREA
Number

RESOURCES
None

GROUP SIZE
Any

IDEA

46

PE MATHS

This is a PE warm-up activity for KS1. During the warm-up, call numbers to elicit the following responses:

o 1 – gentle nods of the head
o 2 – wave arms high above the head
o 3 – hold arms up and stand on one leg
o 4 – lie down on the back and wave arms and legs in the air
o 5 – wiggle the fingers on one hand
o 6 – wiggle the fingers on one hand and gently nod the head
o 7 – wiggle seven fingers
o 8 – wiggle eight fingers
o 9 – wiggle nine fingers
o 10 – wiggle fingers on both hands (or fingers on one hand and toes on one foot).

When the children are accustomed to the responses, put the numbers into a general warm-up activity, calling them at random, e.g. as children are moving around the space, call a number and they have to stop immediately and perform the action before continuing on a signal.

IDEA 47

KEY AREA
Number

RESOURCES
Blank cards
Paper and pencils
Calculators
(optional)

GROUP SIZE
Any

MYSTERY SUMS

Make a bank of questions to consolidate current or previous work which are easily administered by the children themselves.

○ Write questions on blank cards referring to unknown numbers in columns A and B, e.g. Double A × B, A + B, 50% of A + B, (A × 2) + (B × 4). Preserve these as a bank from which the children can choose freely or choose an unseen card at random. Alternatively, they may have to take the top card or they may have a card selected for them.

○ The children make two columns, A and B. Each column contains the numbers 0–9 in random order, thus creating the basis for ten sums.

○ They then choose or receive a question card under the prevailing rules and calculate the resulting sums, i.e. ten sums from the one card.

○ A calculator may be used to check answers if necessary and they can self-mark, or pairs of children can mark each other's.

Example
A child writes 0–9 in columns A and B as below and chooses the card: (A × 2) + (B × 4)

A	B	answer
3	6	6 + 24 = 30
7	0	14 + 0 = 14
6	5	12 + 20 = 32
9	2	18 + 8 = 26
2	4	4 + 16 = 20
0	9	0 + 36 = 36
4	3	8 + 12 = 20
1	1	2 + 4 = 6
8	7	16 + 28 = 44
5	8	10 + 32 = 42

This is a game of deduction.

○ Children sit in a circle and take turns to wear the hat.
○ Write a function and number, such as + 4, on a post-it note and fix it to the hat without the wearer seeing what is on it.
○ Give a number, say 6, which the rest of the group must combine with the hat message and give an answer. For this example the answer would be 10.
○ From the answer, the hat-wearer must guess what is written on the hat. Numbers will often work in more than one way, e.g. if 5 is given to the group and × 6 is on the hat the answer is 30 but the hat-wearer could say, correctly, 'plus 25'. In such cases, either accept any correct answer or press further for the actual one on the hat.
○ The hat is passed on to the next player with a new post-it note, and so on around the group.

DIFFERENTIATION
Vary the post-it notes from simple addition or subtraction to higher number multiplication and division.

KEEP IT ON YOUR HAT

Investigations and longer activities

Most of the ideas in this section are number based but other areas of mathematics are included.

KEY AREA
Number

RESOURCES
Coloured
counters and/or
interlocking
bricks

GROUP SIZE
2–4

This is a counting activity for the younger ones.

○ Spread out an assorted collection of coloured
  counters or interlocking bricks.
○ Ask the children to sort them into their colours and
  then count them into groups of, say, five or ten.
○ Interlocking bricks can be made into columns to
  resemble bar charts.
○ Discuss the colour which has most/least and how
  grouping in quantities helps to count up or see the
  totals.
○ Discuss how the colours can be shared among the
  members of the group.
○ Compare the colour groups and point out
  relationships, e.g. 'There are twice as many yellow as
  red', or 'How many more green than blue are there?'

DIFFERENTIATION

○ Restrict or increase the number of bricks and the
  colour range.

SORTED FOR COLOURS

KEY AREA
Number/shape

RESOURCES
Plastic or card
shapes
Paper and
pencils

GROUP SIZE
Any

IDEA

50

This involves number and shape recognition for KS1
children.

o The children write or trace a large number, say 5, on
  a sheet of paper.
o They then draw groups of [five] shapes, e.g. [five]
  circles, [five] triangles, using card or plastic shapes as
  templates.
o Ask, 'Can we make a set of [five] different shapes?'
  either drawn or chosen from the card/plastic ones.

DIFFERENTIATION
o Vary the number used.
o When complete, ask the child to colour the third,
  fourth or last shape in each set.

NUMBERS SHAPING UP

TEA TIME

KEY AREA
Number
problems

RESOURCES
Plastic tableware
Fruit
Bread
Drinking water
Healthy spread
(optional)

GROUP SIZE
2–4

Here are some real number problems for KS1.

○ Arrange a tea party with three or four friends. The children may like to write invitations to one another.

○ Involve individuals in the group in laying a table with the correct number of plates, cups and cutlery.

○ Assist the children with making a sandwich for everyone in the group, using a half or whole slice of healthy bread per person.

○ Divide the fruit into several pieces – sliced banana, segmented orange or apple – and ask the children to work out how many pieces of each fruit they should have for an equal share. A small box of raisins is a particularly useful inclusion with this as it gives more, individual items.

○ Finally, involve the children in trying to estimate how much water is needed in a jug to give everyone a cupful.

○ When everyone has their ingredients, enjoy the meal.

○ Engage everyone in the cleaning-up operation afterwards.

SAFETY NOTE
Beware of nut and other food allergies. Keep sharp objects out of reach.

KEY AREA	RESOURCES	GROUP SIZE
Money/doubling and addition	Paper and pencils Calculators	Any

This is a KS2 activity which can be used as a class activity or with groups. It aids logical thinking and recording as well as providing practice with doubling.

○ Set a scenario of doing a job, elaborating as much as you wish to on the type of job, with, perhaps, long hours and no breaks. The pay is 2p for the first day, which is doubled for every day after. Ask if anyone would take on the job for, say, four weeks (20 days) and whether it would be worth it.

○ Describe the setting out, using a table:

Day	Pay	Total earned so far
1	2p	2p
2	4p	6p
3	8p	14p
4	16p	30p
5	32p	62p
6	64p	£1.26

and so on to the twentieth day.

○ In the early stages it takes a long time to accumulate wealth but by the time the fifteenth day is reached it is clear that the job is a good one. The final total is £20,971.50 (£5,242.87½ per week).

○ You could suggest they offer to do the washing up at home for four weeks on those terms!

DIFFERENTIATION

○ Some children may manage the calculations without a calculator, but encourage the use of one for checking.

DOUBLE YOUR MONEY

KEY AREA	RESOURCES	GROUP SIZE
Times Tables	Squared paper (cm)	Any
	Card	
	Colouring pencils	
	Glue stick	
	Laminator (optional)	

It is, of course, possible to purchase a tables square but making their own enables children to see patterns in the numbers and how they are interconnected. This design is for tables 2–12 so you will need to reduce the grid size accordingly if you want only 2–10. Actually, the 15× table is a useful one to include due to its association with minutes in an hour.

○ Draw a 12 × 12 grid on 1cm squared paper.
○ Place an × in the top left corner square.
○ Write the numbers 2–12 consecutively from left to right in the squares across the remainder of the top line and from top to bottom in the remainder of the squares in the left-hand column.
○ Colour this column and line in a pastel shade so that the numbers show clearly; these are the key lines.
○ Elicit the 'easiest' table, say the tens, and enter in the values horizontally from the 10 key on the left and vertically from the 10 key at the top, i.e. 20, 30, 40, 50 . . . .
○ Do the same with the next 'easiest' tables in turn, say the twos, fives, elevens, nines and threes.
○ Gradually it can be pointed out that there are not so many gaps in their tables knowledge/expertise as the children may think. These gaps can be filled by careful counting on.
○ Trim the finished squares and mount onto card about 15cm square. Some may like to personalize their square further at this point by giving it a name on the reverse, such as Maths Muncher or Tables Teller.
○ If the finished squares are laminated it will enable constant future use without wear and tear.

○ Use the ready reckoners frequently both as an aid in mathematics lessons and for regular short oral activities. Most children understand readily how this aids multiplication but are unsure of how it can be used for division.

TABLES 4: SQUARE PUZZLES

KEY AREA	RESOURCES	GROUP SIZE
Times tables	Copies of tables squares	Any
	Card	
	Glue	
	Scissors	

Once made, these puzzles can be kept carefully in sets for repeated use.

○ Make photocopies, one per child, of a tables square.
○ Trim off the key horizontal line and vertical column and mount the remainder of the grid onto a square of card exactly the same size.
○ Each child cuts the grid carefully along the squares, in irregular shapes, comprising 4–7 squares, varying the shapes as much as possible. Great care should also be taken so that the children do not mix their own pieces with those of others.
○ Players then swap their set with another child's set and piece the tables square together using clues from the numbers in the lines and columns.

DIFFERENTIATION
Make larger pieces to make the puzzle easier.

KEY AREA
Addition

RESOURCES
Paper and pencils
Calculators

GROUP SIZE
Any

IDEA

55

MAGIC SQUARES

This is an easy way for KS2 children to make magic number squares.

o Explain what makes a magic square, i.e. it is a grid of squares filled with numbers in such a way that each horizontal, vertical and diagonal line adds to the same total.

o Children draw a 3 × 3 grid.

o They choose any number divisible by 3, say 21.

o For this example of 21, 7 (21 ÷ 3) is written in each of the diagonal squares – either direction is OK but only one direction should be used.

o Children then choose two different numbers which total 14 (the difference between 7 and 21), say 9 and 5.

o These are written in the remaining squares in the top line in either order.

o The remaining four squares of the grid are then completed with either 9 or 5 so that each vertical and horizontal line and the remaining diagonal total the 21. There are possible variations with the actual positioning of the numbers, as this example shows:

```
7  5  9      7  9  5      9  5  7      5  9  7
9  7  5      5  7  9      5  7  9      9  7  5
5  9  7      9  5  7      7  9  5      7  5  9
```

This works with any multiple of 3 except 3 itself.

DIFFERENTIATION

o A similar process works with multiples of 4 on a 4 × 4 grid but it is trickier to fit the remaining three numbers in appropriate squares and the second diagonal will not add to the common number.

o It is not necessary to confine this to single-digit numbers on the grid.

o It also works with decimal numbers.

RATIO AND PROPORTION

KEY AREA	RESOURCES	GROUP SIZE
Ratio and proportion	Coloured counters or coloured interlocking bricks	Individually or in pairs

This is a practical way to help with these tricky concepts in upper KS2.

RATIO

○ Children choose a quantity of counters or bricks of just two colours, say, 20 red and 20 green.

○ Separate out one [red] and three [green], explaining that this is in the ratio 1:3.

○ Ask, 'If we wanted two [red] in the same ratio, how many [green] would be needed?'

○ Hopefully, the answer six would result and this can be shown with the counters or bricks, presenting them in clear, separate columns.

○ Now suggest the groupings continue in that presentation until, say, 15 [greens] are coupled with five [red].

○ A pattern might be evident to the children with encouragement and, if appropriate, it can be directly related to the rules of equivalent fractions.

○ Try other ratios, such as 2:5, to consolidate.

PROPORTION

(It is not recommended to cover both ratio and proportion in the same session.)

○ Children take a total of ten counters/bricks, five each of two colours.

○ Show that there are five out of ten [red] and five out of ten [green] and relate it to half are [red] and half are [green], bringing out, if appropriate, the connection with equivalent fractions and, possibly, percentages.

○ Now ask the children to take a total of ten counters/bricks in a random mix of the two colours.

○ Ask, 'How many out of the ten are [red]?' Let's say the answer is six. Then the proportion of [red] counters/bricks is six out of ten. It follows, in this case, that the proportion of [green] counters/bricks is four out of ten.

○ More able children at this point may be happy with discussion on the difference between ratio and proportion.

○ Ask the children to take random amounts of both colours and work out the respective proportions.

DIFFERENTIATION

For a further challenge with either ratio or proportion or both, add a third or fourth colour.

KNOW YOUR ROOTS

KEY AREA	RESOURCES	GROUP SIZE
Square numbers and square roots	A4 1, 5 and 10mm graph paper Rulers Pencils Calculators	Any

One for the more confident children in upper KS2, this activity shows how square numbers plotted on a graph can help with calculations – or close estimates – of square roots and the squares of decimal numbers.

o With a sheet of graph paper in portrait position, children draw x and y axes (arrowed at the ends to indicate that the scales could continue).

o The x axis is numbered on the cm lines from the origin 0 to 15 or as far as it will go and labelled 'Number (square root)'.

o The y axis is numbered on the cm lines from the origin 0 in tens to 200 or as far as it will go and labelled 'Square number'.

o Explain that the graph will begin at the origin as 0^2 is 0.

o Ask the children to plot the squares of all whole numbers and join them to make as smooth a curve as possible.

o Show how, say, 6.8^2, can be calculated by following 6.8 on the x axis up to the drawn line and reading off the answer on the y axis. An accurately drawn and read graph would produce an answer between 45 and 47.

o In reverse, square roots can be shown. Taking $\sqrt{90}$ as an example, follow the 90 line on the y axis to the drawn line and read down to the x axis. In this case, a reasonably accurate answer would be about 9.5.

o Ask children to use the graph to calculate more squares and square roots, checking accuracy on calculators.

KEY AREA	RESOURCES	GROUP SIZE
Number	Two photocopied grids per child (optional) Rulers if children make their own grids Paper and pencils Calculators	Any

These are like a crossword but with numbers and are far easier to make than the wordy relative. It is recommended that a standard grid is produced and copied to make enough for two copies per child. Instead of numbering the clued squares, letters can be used to avoid confusion with the number solutions. If the children make their own it is time consuming and they tend to become confused over the designations of the squares, losing interest by the time the real mathematics begins. A selection of grids would be useful, some larger, allowing for a few four- and five-digit numbers and some smaller, restricting the solutions to two- or three-digit numbers. No solutions should be single-digit numbers.

This is the process once the grids have been produced:

○ The solutions are written on one copy of the grid. The children may have a reason for placing some of the numbers, with particular clues in mind. Others may be numbers placed simply in order to 'fit'. Care should be taken that no solutions begin with a zero. No clues are needed on this grid.

○ The second grid remains blank for another child to complete. The compiler writes clues for the numbers she/he has already placed. Encouragement is needed to provide as many novel and interesting clues as possible but some will inevitably be more straightforward. For example, a solution of 25 could be clued either as 'A quarter of a century' or '5 × 5'.

○ When two people of similar abilities have completed their clues, they swap, each solving the other's puzzle.

Try a 3 × 3 grid without blanked squares. Children make them in the same way, producing just three across clues, A, D and E and three down clues, A, B and C, each solution being a three-digit number. Those who enjoy a challenge could make this type of puzzle on a 4 × 4 grid.

DIFFERENTIATION

Vary the size of the grids, and therefore the size of the numbers in the solution.

KEY AREA
Number

RESOURCES
Paper and pencils

GROUP SIZE
Any

IDEA
59

HUNT THE NUMBER

❍ Search for numbers in the immediate environment and outside. These could be overt as on charts, signs, drain covers and telephone numbers or they could be derived from, say, the number of window panes in a door or the number of fence posts on a given border of the playground. The more obscure the position of the number the greater the value for the searcher.

❍ Formulate questions for such numbers in one of two ways:

a (particularly useful if the numbers are outside) Designate with letters the positions, on a map or simple diagram, where the solutions are to be found. Whether or not solutions need to be found in alphabetical order will need to be decided. A typical example for an entry in this quiz might be, 'Go to point A. What date is engraved on the foundation stone?'

b Direct the players to specific numbers – either to calculate them or simply to find them – and then use those numbers to solve a further problem, such as, 'What is the number of words on the healthy eating poster minus the number of posters in the classroom?'

❍ Alternatively, this could be an investigation of how numbers are used in and around the school with an incentive to find 'the most' or the 'most unusual'.

❍ This activity is far-reaching and can take a while to complete, especially if the children are devising their own questions ready to be presented to another group. An 'award ceremony' could be held at the end to congratulate as many participants as possible for, say, the most correct answers, best thinkers, most sensible searchers, first-to-spot [individual question], most tenacious.

SAFETY NOTE
Assess the level of supervision necessary when the children are working over a wide area inside or outside the building.

KEY AREA
Money

RESOURCES
Store catalogues
Paper and
pencils
Calculators

GROUP SIZE
Any

MAIL ORDER SHOPPING

This is an imaginary way to spend for KS2 children which raises awareness of the cost of items as well as providing practice with calculations.

○ Decide on a theme for spending, depending on the particular catalogues available – sports goods, toys and games, clothing, jewellery. This could vary between groups.

○ Allocate an amount to spend for each group. This will depend to some extent on the cost of items in the given catalogue, e.g. '£200 to be spent on sporting goods'.

○ The children work collaboratively to make a shopping list of desired items, ensuring that they are within the budget and calculating what change, if any, there would be.

○ The final outcome could be presented on a chart, using the illustrations from the catalogue and showing clearly the calculations. Group members could report the reasons for their decisions to buy certain products, such as value for money, necessity or usefulness.

DIFFERENTIATION

○ At its simplest level, ask children to find items in the given category for, say, less than £20.

○ Supplementary challenges could be given in the form of, 'The store has a sale with everything 20% off the catalogue price. What would the cost of the chosen goods then be? What would you do with the savings, remembering that any additional items would also be 20% off?'

Times tables/line graphs

Rulers
Pencils
A4 1, 5 and
10mm graph
paper (cm
squared paper
can be used but
it is not so
accurate for
reading
multiplications
and divisions)

Any

TABLES 5: GRAPHS

This KS2 activity shows how times tables plotted on a graph result in a straight line. The gradient varies with each table – the higher the table the steeper the gradient. It also shows that multiplication and division can be calculated from the lines produced – or a very close estimate.

○ With a sheet of graph paper in portrait position, children draw x and y axes (arrowed at the ends to indicate that the scales could continue).

○ The x axis is numbered on the cm lines from the origin 0 to 15 or as far as it will go and labelled 'Times'.

○ The y axis is numbered on the cm lines from the origin 0 in tens to 200 or as far as it will go and labelled 'Multiples'.

○ Explain that all the tables will begin at the origin as 0 times any number is 0.

○ Use a times table as an example, say, the fives and ask the children to plot 10 × 5 on the graph – following the ten times line up from the x axis until it meets the 50 multiple line across from the y axis.

○ To be sure, plot also the 5 × 5 (where 5 from the x meets 25 from the y).

○ A ruler is aligned through the two points and the origin – which should be in a straight line – and a line drawn from the zero through the two points and right to the edge of the paper.

○ Show how multiplication of 5 and division by 5 can be calculated using the line, e.g. for 14 × 5 follow the 14 line up from the x axis until it meets the drawn line, read across from that point to the y axis which should be 70. And for 43 ÷ 5 follow the 43 line across from the y axis until it meets the drawn line, read down from that point to the x axis which should be 8.6 or very close.

○ Other tables can now be plotted using the same procedure with the known amounts of ten times and five times together with the origin. If several different tables are plotted on the same sheet of paper, it will clearly show the comparative gradients. Children must remember to label each line with the respective table.

○ The lines can be used to calculate some tricky multiplication and division questions.

DIFFERENTIATION

Lower ability children will need considerable help.

KEY AREA	RESOURCES	GROUP SIZE
Number	Isometric paper and cm squared paper	Any
	Cubes	

Use this upper KS2 activity to investigate triangle, square and cube numbers, not necessarily altogether.

○ Triangle numbers – set out the triangle numbers, using isometric paper (or squared paper held at 45°). Ask the children to find the sequence produced in any direction, i.e. the differences between diagonal numbers run consecutively in any diagonal direction.

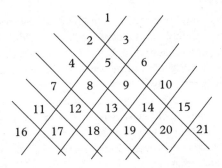

○ Square numbers – on cm squared paper, ask the children to outline a single square which represents 1 × 1 or $1^2 = 1$. Follow with a 2 × 2 square which gives four squares in all. Continue with other square numbers in order which results in a sequence of: 1, 4, 9, 16, 25, 36, 49 and so on.

○ Cube numbers – the cube, being 3D is 1 × 1 × 1 = 1^3. Children add cubes to give a shape 2 × 2 × 2 which produces a solid of eight cubes. Ask them to continue with 3 × 3 × 3 and so on to produce the cube sequence: 1, 8, 27, 64, 125, 216. It is not suggested that they use that many cubes but it will be seen by 27 that the numbers increase rapidly.

DIFFERENTIATION

Only the more able will attempt the cube numbers.

TRIANGLE, SQUARE, CUBE

IDEA

63

THE LITTLE BOOK OF NUMBERS

KEY AREA
Number

RESOURCES
A4 plain paper
Rulers
Pencils and
colouring pencils

GROUP SIZE
Any – some
children may
prefer to work in
collaborative
groups

This useful, creative project for all ages can be picked up
and put down as time permits. The object is to create a
book about numbers. A folded sheet of A4 paper
produces four pages. Children decide how many pages
they need to place together as a book at the outset. This
is important because the numbers will need to be
consecutive in most cases. The following are merely
suggestions.

○ A counting book, which could be made by the
youngest children as a class book or by older children
for a younger audience. It would have a theme, such
as 'Mrs Pringle did some washing. She washed one
sheet (page 1), two shirts (page 2), three jumpers
(page 3)' and so on, up to about ten.

○ The theme could be simply dots or sweets or animals.
The children may well do some of their own artwork,
but stickers are a very useful means of producing
repeated images.

○ Another theme could be shapes, the numbers
representing the number of sides, i.e. 1 for 'circle', 2
for 'semi-circle', 3 for 'triangle' and so on.

○ Older children may like to make a short story centred
around sums, such as, 'Mrs Crumble, the baker,
made 50 cream buns. The Mayor bought half of them
for a party (page 1). Mr Jackson bought one each for
his family of five (page 2). Ten went to the lady next
door for her coffee morning (page 3). Eight men from
the building site had one each for lunch (page 4). A
couple bought one each to take to the park (page 5).
How many did that leave for me? (page 6). Oh,
crumbs! (page 7).

○ This project lends itself readily to computer
presentations.

VARIATION
A slightly different kind of book could be centred around time, looking at units of time from seconds to centuries and millennia, at the amount of time spent on various activities or at the times of day.

KEY AREA
Times
tables/number
patterns

RESOURCES
Paper and pencils

GROUP SIZE
Any

Patterns can be obtained from all of the times tables and the object of this activity is for the children to find them and investigate links between the various tables.

o Explain that if the digits of the answers in a table are added, a pattern will be produced.
o Demonstrate the process with the nine times table:

9 becomes 9
18 is 1 + 8 = 9
27 is 2 + 7 = 9
36 is 3 + 6 = 9
45 is 4 + 5 = 9
54 is 5 + 4 = 9 and so on to 10 × or 12 ×.

N.B: If the result of any addition is a two-digit number, these digits must then be added to produce a single digit, thus 49 in the seven times table is 4 + 9 = 13 then 1 + 3 = 4.

o Point out that the nine times table is the only table which produces a single-number pattern in this way. The others have patterns which are more difficult to spot. It is also worth mentioning that the pattern can be used to test divisibility by 9, i.e. if the digits of the number eventually make 9 then the number is divisible by 9, so 4,502,187 is divisible by 9 because 4 + 5 + 0 + 2 + 1 + 8 + 7 = 27 and 2 + 7 = 9.

o Set an investigation to discover the patterns in any or all of the other tables using the same process (it may be necessary to begin a second table to secure the method). It is beneficial for the children to work collaboratively with this.

o These are the patterns derived:

Twos – 2, 4, 6, 8, 1, 3, 5, 7, 9, 2, 4, 6 and so on
Threes – 3, 6, 9, 3, 6, 9, 3, 6, 9, 3, 6, 9
Fours – 4, 8, 3, 7, 2, 6, 1, 5, 9, 4, 8, 3 (numbers decrease by 1 in pairs)
Fives – 5, 1, 6, 2, 7, 3, 8, 4, 9, 5, 1, 6 (numbers increase by 1 in pairs)

Sixes – 6, 3, 9, 6, 3, 9, 6, 3, 9, 6, 3, 9

Sevens – 7, 5, 3, 1, 8, 6, 4, 2, 9, 7, 5, 3 (numbers decrease alternately odds and evens)

Eights – 8, 7, 6, 5, 4, 3, 2, 1, 9, 8, 7, 6

Nines – as above

Tens – 1, 2, 3, 4, 5, 6, 7, 8, 9, 1, 2, 3

Elevens – 2, 4, 6, 8, 1, 3, 5, 7, 9, 2, 4, 6 (numbers increase alternately evens and odds)

Twelves – 3, 6, 9, 3, 6, 9, 3, 6, 9, 3, 6, 9

Fifteens – 6, 3, 9, 6, 3, 9, 6, 3, 9, 6, 3, 9

○ A second part of the investigation is to consider similarities between the tables, e.g. the threes, sixes, twelves and fifteens, the twos and fours, the fives and tens.

DIFFERENTIATION

Some children may want to try higher tables, e.g. the sixteens or seventeens.

IDEA 65

KEY AREA	RESOURCES	GROUP SIZE
Probability	Dice	Any
	Paper and pencils	

This investigation for KS2 looks at the reasons for always buying the orange properties when playing Monopoly.

Single dice
○ Begin by discussing the probability of throwing any of the six numbers on a single dice, i.e. one in six.
○ Working in pairs, children can test the theory by throwing, say, 50 times and recording how many of each number were cast.
○ Results can be collated from other pairs for an overall conclusion.

Two dice
○ Discuss the ways of obtaining all possible scores in the conventional, adding-the-spots, sense.

Score	Number of ways	Possible throws
1	0	impossible
2	1	double 1
3	1	2 + 1
4	2	3 + 1/double 2
5	2	3 + 2/4 + 1
6	3	5 + 1/4 + 2/double 3
7	3	6 + 1/5 + 2/4 + 3
8	3	6 + 2/5 + 3/double 4
9	2	6 + 3/5 + 4
10	2	6 + 4/double 5
11	1	6 + 5
12	1	double 6

○ It will be concluded that there is a greater probability of throwing 6, 7 or 8 compared to the other possible scores.
○ Test the theory in the same way as the test for the single dice and discuss the results.
○ Purely for interest value it could be pointed out that the orange properties in a game of Monopoly are the best ones to buy, even more than the four sets of the highest face value. The reasons for this are the

likelihood of landing on the orange properties after being in 'Jail' (two of the orange set are six and eight squares away from the jail respectively) and the number of opportunities of landing on the 'Jail' square – just landing on it, or being sent there (Chance/Community Chest/Go To Jail).

PROBABILITY: CARDS

KEY AREA
Probability

RESOURCES
Playing cards
Paper and pencils

GROUP SIZE
Any

This game for KS2 children is great fun and keeps the mind active, but it can be a bit frustrating to operate until the players are accustomed to it. Using half the cards from a pack provides greater chances of points and the game is completed more quickly, but it is still successful with a whole pack.

○ Use one red and one black suit, say, hearts and clubs. Shuffle and place them in a pile, face down.

○ Discuss the possibilities of what the top card might be and compare the chances of it being: a red card; a black card, a court card, an even/odd number; a high/low card (above/below 7); a specific card, such as a 7. The game requires players to make guesses on what each turn of the card might be. Points are scored depending on how likely it is that particular cards will/might turn up. Thus: a 50/50 chance like a red card would score only one or two points if correct; a roughly one in four chance of a picture card would give about five points; a slim chance like an ace could score ten points.

○ Decide the range of possible guesses and agree abbreviations which will enable a fast-moving game. B = black, R = red, P = picture, HB/HR = high black/red, LB/LR = low black/red, A = ace.

○ Players make a table with three columns headed 'Guess', 'Actual' and 'Points'.

○ Once everyone is clear on how many points are scored for respective correct guesses they write in their first guess.

○ The top card is turned and announced. Those with a correct guess score the relevant points, keeping their own score, e.g. if the card turned is 9 of clubs a B guess scores two, an HB guess scores four, a B9 guess scores ten. Those guessing LB, HR, LR, R, P or any other specific card score nothing.

○ Players write down their guesses for the next card and so the game progresses.

○ Each card turned is placed in view so that players can adjust their opinion on future possibilities based on the number of high/low/black/red cards that have been revealed.

○ At some point, about ten cards into the game, introduce a 'bonus' round in which all regular guesses are suspended. Select a card which has not yet surfaced, say, the ace of hearts and offer ten points for it not being that ace or 20 points if it is. The players should select Y or N in their guess column. This can be repeated for suitable selections further on.

○ When there are eventually only two or three cards remaining, it may well be obvious what the choices and chances of a correct guess would be and here the points offered could be raised for extra excitement and interest.

DIFFERENTIATION

Reduce the guessing possibilities to play the game at a lower level, e.g. a simple choice between red and black or red/black/picture.

KEY AREA
Averages/data
handling

RESOURCES
Photocopies of
short texts aimed
at a range of ages
Paper and pencils
Calculators

GROUP SIZE
2–4

LETTERS AND WORDS: THE MEAN, MODE AND MEDIAN

Maths meets literature in this full-scale investigation for upper KS2. In advance, prepare photocopies of reading texts from about four different reading ages, ranging from very early readers to about age 10 or 11. Enlargements will make the work of counting much easier. Use the same number of words for each text, say 20.

Groups should work cooperatively, sharing the different photocopies among them and pooling their individual results for a final conclusion.

The mean is an average obtained by division of the total by the number of items in the list. The mode is the most often occurring value. The median is the middle value in a list ordered from smallest to largest.

o For each of the copies, find the mode, median and mean word length.
o For each of the copies, find the most frequently occurring letter/s.

For the word length task, the children:

o construct a frequency chart to tally the number of words with different numbers of letters
o arrange the results in order to find the mode and median, remembering that, if it is a 20-word text, then the median will be the difference between the tenth and eleventh in the series
o total the number of letters and divide by the number of words to calculate the mean.

For the commonest letter/s task, the children:

○ construct a frequency chart to tally the numbers of
  each of the letters
○ present the results in the form of a bar chart
○ attempt to calculate the ratio of vowels to consonants.

At the end of the investigation, the groups should agree
on a conclusion, comparing word length and letter usage
in books intended for younger and older readers.

DIFFERENTIATION
Ensure that the less able are supported and given
meaningful tasks within any cooperative group.

Measures and time

Here are 17 practical ideas to support this often complex and tricky area of mathematics.

MORE OR LESS CENTIMETRES

KEY AREA	RESOURCES	GROUP SIZE
Linear measurement	Rulers A2 sheets of paper Range of readily available items as listed in text	Any

○ Prepare a chart of three columns on a sheet of A2 paper. The column headings should read from left to right: 'less than 10cm'; 'exactly 10cm'; 'more than 10cm'.

○ Spread out a number of items, some of which are clearly more or less than 10cm in length and some which will need measurement to check, e.g. pencil sharpener, scissors, calculator, pencil, paintbrush, rubber, plastic cup, pencil case. Include some lengths of string and strips of paper or cloth.

○ Set the task to place the selected items in the correct columns, either physically or writing or drawing them in.

○ At an appropriate time, suggest producing items exactly 10cm long from string or paper.

DIFFERENTIATION

○ Younger or less able children could simply arrange the items in order of length.

○ For older or more able children, make the 'exact' measurement more precise, e.g. 10.7cm, and require them to include the exact measurements on the chart.

This is a new twist on the old game.

o Players sit in a circle or around a table and take turns to be Mr Wolf.

o The first Mr Wolf secretly sets a time on her/his own clock and the rest of the group chant, 'What's the time, Mr Wolf?'

o The designated player says the time she/he has made without showing it, and the rest of the group make that time on their clocks.

o When all the players have set a time, they are checked and any with an incorrect time are metaphorically eaten (including Mr Wolf, if her/his time is wrong) with the expression, 'Gobble, gobble, yum, yum.'

o Play then passes to the next Mr Wolf.

DIFFERENTIATION

It is essential that groups consist of members with similar time-telling abilities, in order to maintain enjoyment for all.

o At the game's simplest level, times might be restricted to 'o'clock' and 'half-past'.

o The advanced game would include minutes, digital/analogue terminology and 24-hour clock times.

WHAT'S THE TIME, MR WOLF?

A NEW ANGLE

KEY AREA	RESOURCES	GROUP SIZE
Angles	Prepared sheet of angles	Any
	Gummed paper or coloured paper and glue	
	Scissors	
	Protractors (for the older children's version)	

This involves a slightly different approach to recognizing and constructing angles.

Make a sheet for photocopying of about ten angles, in a range of acute and obtuse, including a reflex angle or two for older children. They do not have to be measured.

For younger children
o Ask the children to look at each angle in turn, estimate it and try to repeat it on the gummed/coloured paper.
o The attempt is then cut out and placed into its photocopied counterpart.
o Under- and over-estimations are discussed in order to improve accuracy for later attempts.
o Older children will be able to recognize which of the angles are acute and which are obtuse.

For older children
o Older children will enjoy the guessing version and this can be encouraged as long as there is also practice with the protractors.
o Use photocopies including reflex angles if the children are familiar with that concept.
o Children use a protractor to measure each angle in turn.
o This angle is then reproduced on the gummed/ coloured paper and stuck on the photocopy.
o The angle measurements should be written inside their respective angles.

KEY AREA	RESOURCES	GROUP SIZE
Linear	Metre wheel	2–4
measurement/	Metre sticks	
area	Calculators	
	Paper and pencils	

IDEA

71

Choose from this pick-and-mix list of practical ideas for measuring in the playground and ask the children to try some:

o Estimate the length and width of the playground itself.
o Use a metre wheel to measure the length and width.
o Pace out the length and width and from this calculate the average length of one pace.
o Compare length of walking pace with length of running pace.
o Find the average height of people in the class and calculate how many would fit head to toe from one end of the playground to the other.
o Calculate the area (either the main rectangular section or inclusive of additional parts).
o Estimate how many people could stand reasonably comfortably in the area.
o Calculate how many school tables could be placed in the area.
o Measure the perimeter.

DIFFERENTIATION
Adapt activities to suit age and ability.

SAFETY NOTE
Assess the supervision level required for working outside.

PLAYGROUND MEASURES

KEY AREA
Angle
measurements

RESOURCES
Plain paper
Rulers
Compasses
Protractors

GROUP SIZE
Any

TWICE AS SHARP: BISECTING ANGLES

This upper KS2 activity is a simple procedure providing practice with compasses and protractors. Demonstrate the method for the children to follow:

○ Draw an angle, either acute or obtuse. There is no need at this point to measure it but it should not be too acute.

○ Measure the same distance from the point along each line, say, 3cm and make a mark.

○ Set the compasses at a comfortable radius, the actual opening does not matter. With the compass point on one of the measured marks, draw an arc across the opening of the angle.

○ Without altering the radius of the compasses, make the arc into a 'cross' from the second measured mark.

○ A line through the centre of the cross to the angle point bisects the angle.

○ Check by measuring the resulting angles with a protractor.

○ Try this with other angles. It also works with reflex angles.

○ If time permits, encourage experimentation with design, based on the principle of bisecting angles.

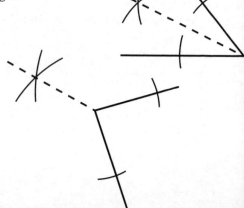

KEY AREA
Volume

RESOURCES
Various small
cartons and cm
cubes

GROUP SIZE
Any

IDEA

73

An introduction to the concept of volume.

○ Show a carton and a cm cube and ask for an estimate
of how many cubes would fit into the carton: a)
haphazardly and b) uniformly.
○ Children carry out the task to check their estimates,
first filling the carton by putting in three or four at a
time randomly, then taking care to align them as
tightly as possible.
○ Using their knowledge of the first carton, children
then estimate for other cartons before again checking.
○ If appropriate, relate the numbers of cubes in the
carton to a calculation of length × width × height.

CUBES IN A BOX

KEY AREA
Time

RESOURCES
Timer
Game requires
a hall or
playground

GROUP SIZE
Any (works well
with large
numbers)

MINUTE WALK

This game helps with estimation and judgement of time and is useful as a party game if there is plenty of space.

○ Mark out start and finish lines at opposite ends of a hall or playground area.

○ Players line up at the start.

○ At a given signal they walk in a straight line to the finish in exactly one minute.

○ Hands are kept behind backs to avoid looking at watches.

○ The speed each player starts at must be kept reasonably constant. Any players hovering at the finishing line are disqualified.

○ As players cross the finishing line they are out.

○ The winner is the player on or nearest (but not over) the finishing line when the minute is up.

KEY AREA
Measurement

RESOURCES
Pack of exercise
books
Reading book
Box of paper
clips
Scales
Rulers
Calculators

GROUP SIZE
Any

IDEA
75

PROBLEM MEASURES

Here are some posers for upper KS2.

○ Discuss the task of finding the thickness of an exercise book and seek possible solutions.

○ Eventually suggest – if the idea has not already been offered – measuring a pack of exercise books and dividing by the number in the pack.

○ Carry out the task.

○ Follow up with a quest to find the width of a sheet of paper by measuring a reading book and dividing by the number of pages. Remember that there are always a few unnumbered pages and, as the pages are numbered on both sides, the final page number needs to be halved.

○ Transfer the process to finding the weight of a single paperclip, using an unopened box of 500. Similarly, the weight of a single elastic band might be found. Don't forget the weight of the carton. Reversing the process, it is possible to make an accurate estimate of the length of line which could be made by every person in the school standing arms outstretched, touching fingertips. For a rough estimate, measure an average child from the class in the 'pose' and multiply by the number of people in the school.

○ For a more accurate estimate, collect the measurements of Miss or Master Average from every year group, divide by the number of children concerned and then multiply by the total school population. The children may suggest other lengths and weights to explore in this way.

KEY AREA
Time/data handling

RESOURCES
Pre-watershed pages of television and radio listings

GROUP SIZE
Any

TV TIMES

Use an important influence in our lives to fuel a timely investigation with KS2 children. The programme pages of television and radio listings are a good source of real-life questions for calculating time differences for individual programmes, collective groups of programmes and waiting times.

If a longer-term activity is called for, help the children to devise an investigation of their own or construct one for them. It may be advisable to confine the investigation to one or two channels. Here are some ideas:

o Compare the length of time for factual TV programmes across a week's viewing and discover the popular and less popular days for them.

o Make similar studies of films, programmes about animals or with animals as central characters, children's television, comedy.

o Try to work out the amount of TV time taken up by American productions on any given day or on a weekly basis.

o Carry out a pupil survey of favourite programmes and present the results in graph form combined with further information and artwork about them.

o Compare TV timings with radio programmes.

o Compare radio channels for their talk/music content.

KEY AREA
Capacity

RESOURCES
Clean plastic
measuring
cylinder or
empty litre
plastic bottle
Plastic funnel
Identical plastic
cups
Access to
drinking water
Calculators

GROUP SIZE
2–4

**IDEA
77**

WHAT IS A CUPFUL?

This is a KS2 investigation. Be prepared for water spillage. If fresh water is used in clean containers it can be drunk after the investigation, thus avoiding waste and promoting a healthy activity.

○ Ensure knowledge of 1,000ml = 1 litre.
○ Children estimate how many cups of water can be poured from a measured litre.
○ Once all estimates are made, an empty litre measuring cylinder or litre plastic bottle is filled one cupful at a time, using a plastic funnel. Care must be taken to record the exact numbers of cups used and the fraction, if any, of the final one.
○ Elicit the calculation, 1,000 ÷ (number of cups plus any fraction) in order to arrive at the number of ml per cup.

DIFFERENTIATION
○ Younger children can do this simply as an estimation of capacity, comparing different shaped containers, without involving numerical calculations.
○ Challenge with a subsidiary problem, such as, 'How many cups would fill a two-litre/five-litre container?' or 'How could I measure out 600ml as accurately as possible using only these cups?'

KEY AREA	RESOURCES	GROUP SIZE
Timetables	Squared paper Maps of the local area and further afield	Any

Often bus and train timetable questions in schools are made up from imaginary towns and mileages. Try tackling the concept from the local area by helping the children to construct their own timetables based on real life. This is a challenging upper KS2 activity which combines mathematics with geography.

Demonstrate how to make a grid for a timetable or provide blank grids. Alternatively, the children could do this on the 'table' facility of a computer or on a spreadsheet program.

Children carry out the task in the following steps:

○ Decide if the timetable is to be for bus or train.
○ Use a map of the local area and decide on the termini.
○ Write in the terminus and the departure time for the first outward journey of the day.
○ Using the map again, write in several stops on the way to the final destination.
○ Estimate, given the comparative distances between stops, the times of arrival/departure and write them in for the first outward journey. These times do not have to be totally realistic. The time lapses can vary depending on the ability of the children concerned, but children should be encouraged to include odd minutes rather than just 15-minute, half-hourly or hourly intervals.
○ Add further buses/trains for the route at realistic intervals during the day or part-day. Again, avoid hourly or half-hourly intervals if possible.

DIFFERENTIATION

○ More or fewer journeys can be constructed with more regular and more easily calculated time intervals.
○ More able children may like to consider express buses/trains which omit certain stops.

This is for upper KS2 children.

○ Get the children to draw a faint base line, say, 16cm long, and mark the mid-point.

○ A protractor is set on the mid-point and every 10° from 0–180° is marked.

○ The design can be built up by deciding the length of lines drawn from the mid-point of the original line to the 10° markers or beyond. Not all the 10° markers need to be used. Lines can continue below the original line if desired.

○ Once the chosen radials have been drawn, the ends can be joined with straight lines or arcs to complete the design.

○ A ruler is aligned between a 10° mark and the centre point. Children then draw a measured line through the 10° mark to the centre point and beyond the same distance below the original line.

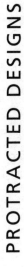

PROTRACTED DESIGNS

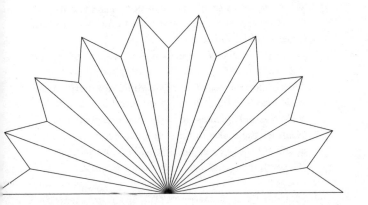

KEY AREA
Imperial/metric
conversion
graphs

RESOURCES
Metre rules
Dual-graduated
inch/cm ruler
Graph paper

GROUP SIZE
Any

Many children still consider their height in feet and inches and find it difficult to relate it to metres and centimetres. Here is an opportunity to capitalize on their enjoyment of being measured and cover the concept of conversion at the same time. Although the recording and presentation of the measurements is more suited to KS2, younger children like to be involved with measuring each other as a practical exercise.

○ Discuss how people measure their height and ascertain if the children know how tall they are. Demonstrate differences between metric and imperial units on a dual-graduated inch/cm ruler, showing that 30cm is approximately 12 inches or one foot.

○ Explain that the expected units of length measurement are mm, cm, m and km and a conversion graph is one way of moving between metric and imperial distances.

Demonstrate how to draw the conversion graph:

○ With a sheet of graph paper in portrait position, draw x and y axes (arrowed at the ends to indicate that the scales could continue).

○ Number the x axis in ones on alternate cm lines from the origin 0 to 7 or as far as it will go and label it 'Feet'. Explain the division of whole numbers on this scale into 12 inches to the foot, using 3, 6 and 9 inches as benchmarks of ¼, ½ and ¾ respectively.

○ Number the y axis in tens on the cm lines from the origin 0 to 200 or as far as it will go and label it 'Centimetres (cm)' and adding in the 1m and 2m marks.

○ Plot the 1 foot/30cm point and, as a check, 2 feet/ 60cm.

○ Align a ruler through the two points and the origin –
  which should be in a straight line – and draw a line
  from the zero through the two points and right to the
  edge of the paper.
○ Show how measurements in metric and imperial can
  be converted (within the range drawn) using this line.

Explain how height can be measured:

○ Stand (shoes on or off) against a whiteboard with 1
  metre from the ground already marked. Use a ruler to
  set a horizontal line from the top of the head to the
  whiteboard and place a mark. Add the distance above
  the metre mark for the total height.
○ Lie down on a long sheet of paper, taking care to
  allow for the curve of the head when making a mark.
○ Use a custom-made height gauge.

Children pair up to measure each other's height with
appropriate adult support and construct the conversion
graphs. They will then be able to convert their own
heights to approximate feet and inches. Any who already
knew their height in imperial units can check in metric,
using the conversion graph.

There is scope for a considerable amount of further
work with measuring other parts of the body, such as
head circumference, hand span, cubit, length of foot, and
converting these to imperial.

KEY AREA
Mass

RESOURCES
Sand
Plastic bricks
Polythene bags
Scales (spring
balance, balance
and kitchen
scales if possible)

GROUP SIZE
Any

Demonstrate variations between quantity and mass.

o Discuss the weight of various familiar items, how we estimate weight, and the types of scales available.

o Set the task to estimate 250g of sand and 250g of plastic bricks, placing each quantity in equal-sized polythene bags.

o Weigh the bags to check the estimates, using as many different types of scales as possible.

o Children should record their plus or minus difference between the actual weight and their estimates, before adjusting by adding or removing amounts to achieve exactly 250g.

o If working with a full class, it would be interesting to collect some data, such as which of the plastic bricks and sand was easiest to estimate and possible reasons why; what were the closest and furthest estimates for both?

o With an accurately weighed 250g quantity of plastic bricks, can the weight of a single brick be calculated?

KEY AREA
Measurement

RESOURCES
Whiteboards and
pens

GROUP SIZE
3–6 similar
ability

IDEA

82

Children collaborate to consolidate the terminology of units of measurement in KS2. Players in this game must be familiar with the facts and concepts of: 1 litre = 1,000ml; 1kg = 1,000g; 1 metre = 1,000mm; 1km = 1,000m.

○ Players take turns to set a question for the rest of the group which takes the form of a quantity, e.g. 2kg 500g.

○ The other players must write the quantity in a different way – in this example, either 2½ kg or 2.5kg. The group works cooperatively to ensure everyone has an acceptable notation.

DIFFERENTIATION
The more confident will enjoy operating this game independently. Generally, groups of similar ability will find their own level of complexity.

THE THOUSAND TO ONE GAME

CALENDAR OF CALENDARS

KEY AREA
Time (calendars)

RESOURCES
Photocopied/
printed sheets

GROUP SIZE
Pairs

This helps KS2 children improve familiarity with calendars and dates. The 'clerical side' of this activity – once the pro forma has been produced – is the responsibility of the children themselves, working on a rota.

Prepare a daily recording sheet as simply or elaborately as you wish for a rota of pairs of children to complete. Include any or all of the following:

○ Today's date
○ The date one week ago
○ The date one week from now
○ The weather conditions
○ Today is special because . . . (e.g. birthdays, Saint's day, No Smoking Day)
○ On this day in history . . . (there are good websites available for this).

Points of interest related to any given day can be discussed at an appropriate time.

DIFFERENTIATION
Encourage the children to assist each other.

KEY AREA
Time

RESOURCES
Blank cards
Felt pens

GROUP SIZE
Teams of 4–6

IDEA

84

This time challenge for KS2 is a team game. Team members can confer but they should be encouraged to take turns with answering. In this example, teams of five will translate analogue to digital times and vice versa.

○ Each member of team A writes an analogue time on a card, e.g. 20 past 3 p.m. or, in full, 'twenty past three in the afternoon'. Team B has [5] blank cards and must not see what team A has written.

○ Team A then reads out the cards in turn, allowing team B to write the corresponding digital times on their blank cards.

○ Team B then reads each time they have written in digital to team A in turn. Team A show the matching analogue times as they are read. Accurate matches go to team B and incorrect matches go to team A. A 'referee' should be on hand to settle disputes over accuracy.

○ The game continues with the teams' roles reversed.

This game also works well with translating analogue/digital times to the 24-hour clock.

DIFFERENTIATION
Opposing teams should be evenly matched in ability as far as possible.

ANALOGUE V DIGITAL

Shape, space and design

These final 16 ideas capitalize on children's enjoyment of exploring shape but take it further to extend manipulative and design skills. Some incorporate the investigational with the creative while promoting greater accuracy and a sense of achievement.

KEY AREA
Shape

RESOURCES
Art materials
Examples of
shapes
Gummed shapes
(optional)

GROUP SIZE
Any

MR SQUARE AND MRS CIRCLE

This is an activity for KS1 and lower KS2.

Talk about shapes and show examples. Point out shapes in pictures, such as bicycle wheels, houses, and rooftops. Tell the story of Mr Square:

o 'Mr Square lives in a square house. He has a square garden with a square tree and square flowers. He has a square dog called Boxy and he drives a square car.' Perhaps the children can add other square things in Mr Square's life.

o Ask the children to make a picture of Mr Square and some of the things mentioned in the story. If you have sets of different sized stick-on shapes this would make this task easier and more accurate.

o The same treatment can be given to Mrs Circle, Miss Triangle and Mr Star, remembering that the gender and marital status can be anything.

o The children can choose which shape to use in their picture but encourage them to concentrate on a single shape rather than making a picture containing random squares, circles, triangles and stars.

o Alternatively, the children could make a 'person-only' group of, say, Mr Square, Mrs Star, Miss Circle and Little Baby Triangle.

DIFFERENTIATION
Older children may like to make a shape story book for the younger ones.

KEY AREA
Shape

RESOURCES
Plastic or card
2D shapes
Large hoops
(could be drawn
on A3 paper)

GROUP SIZE
2–4

I D E A

86

This is a shape-learning activity for KS1.

○ Place two large hoops, overlapping in the middle.
  Alternatively mark out circles on a sheet of A3 paper.
○ Label one circle, say, 'Squares' (drawing a square
  alongside to assist) and the other 'Red shapes'
  (written in red).
○ Spread out a selection of plastic or card 2D shapes
  and support the children with placing them in the
  correct sections of the Venn diagram, i.e. all the
  squares, except the red ones, would be in the
  'Squares' section, all red shapes in the other section,
  but red squares should be in the overlapped section.
○ Vary the specified shape to include circles, triangles,
  oblongs/rectangles, and so on.
○ This can also be used for 3D shapes.

VENN SHAPES

KEY AREA
Shape

RESOURCES
Large selection
of plastic or card
2D shapes

GROUP SIZE
2–4

FOLLOW MY SHAPE

Play this shape-learning game with KS1 children.

o Share out the 2D shapes so that each child has an assortment of 15–20.

o Nominate a child to place one shape in the middle of the table.

o Subsequent players lay the same shape but it can be a different colour or size.

o The starting player then lays a different shape for play to continue in the same way.

o If any player cannot go, she/he becomes the new starter for others to follow with the same shape, albeit a different colour or size.

This game also works well with 3D shapes.

KEY AREA	RESOURCES	GROUP SIZE
2D and 3D shapes	Card or plastic 2D and 3D shapes Tray for each group	Pairs, threes or fours

This is the traditional Kim's Game, using shapes as the theme.

o Spread about 10 or 12 shapes on a tray. They could be all 2D, all 3D or a mixture. Some could be duplicated but different sizes or colours.

o The players have a given amount of time to memorize the selection before it is removed from sight.

o One of the shapes is secretly taken from the selection before it is presented to the players again.

o The players then have to deduce which shape has been removed.

o Clues can be given in cases of difficulty by indicating properties of the shape removed.

DIFFERENTIATION
Vary the number and complexity of the shapes according to age and ability.

COMPLETE THE CIRCLE

KEY AREA
Shape

RESOURCES
Gummed or self-adhesive circles

GROUP SIZE
Any

This activity improves familiarity with circles at all levels of ability.

Tip: To find the centre of a paper circle, fold it in two positions. The point at which the diameter-creases cross is the centre.

Elementary
○ Cut various sized segments of no particular measurements from several gummed circles.
○ Put the segments to one side for later use and stick the remaining parts of the circles onto paper.
○ Children then place the cut segments into the correct spaces. Encourage estimation on which segments belong in which spaces prior to placing.

Intermediate
○ Cut various sized segments of no particular measurements from several gummed circles.
○ Put the segments to one side for later use and stick the remaining parts of the circles onto paper.
○ For each circle, ask for estimates of the fraction which has been removed and the fraction remaining.

Advanced
○ Cut various sized segments of no particular measurements from several gummed circles.
○ Put the segments to one side for later use and stick the remaining parts of the circles onto paper.
○ For each circle, ask for an estimate of the angle of the segment made from the centre and then an accurate measurement of that angle.
○ Cover the fraction concept as in the intermediate activity and relate it to pie charts, giving numerical examples, e.g. (for a segment fraction of one-fifth) 'In a group of 30 people, the favourite sport of [this segment] was swimming. How many people liked swimming best?'

KEY AREA
Construction of
shape

RESOURCES
Compasses
Protractors
Pencils
Rulers

GROUP SIZE
Any

IDEA

90

CIRCLES TAKING SHAPES

This upper KS2 activity involves drawing regular
polygons in a circle. Any regular 2D shape can be drawn
using a circle as a guide – simply calculate $360° \div$
number of sides.

○ Children draw a circle with a radius of approximately
6cm, ensuring that the centre will be easily found.
○ A protractor is aligned to the centre of the circle on a
faintly drawn horizontal diameter. The procedure for
using a 180° protractor is given here as they are the
popular choice. If a 360° protractor is used, the
diameter line is not actually needed.
○ The required angles for the chosen shape are then
marked off, see below.
○ Children draw a faint line from the centre, through
the angle marks, to the circumference. Actually, all
that is required is a dot on the circumference but
many children are more comfortable drawing the line.
○ The dots are then joined in turn around the
circumference with a heavy straight line and the shape
appears.

Explain how to make the shapes with their
corresponding angles:

○ Equilateral triangle – 120°, turn the 180° protractor
to the other half of the circle and mark 60°. The third
mark will be at 180°.
○ Square – use the diameter already drawn, mark 90°
and draw a faint vertical diameter.
○ Pentagon – mark: 0°, 72°, 144°, turn the protractor
to the other half and mark: 36°, 108°.

- Hexagon – mark: 0°, 60°, 120°, 180°, which is enough if each mark is used to draw a faint diameter.
- Heptagon (this is the trickiest but it does produce the shape of a 50p or 20p piece) – mark: 0°, 51°, 103°, 154°, turn the protractor to the other half and mark: 26°, 77°, 129°. The divisions for this shape are not precise, of course, but it is probably as close as it can be.
- Octagon – mark: 0°, 45°, 90°, 135°, 180°, which is enough if each mark is used to draw a faint diameter.
- Nonagon – mark: 0°, 40°, 80°, 120°, 160°, turn the protractor to the other half and mark: 20°, 60°, 100°, 140°.
- Decagon – mark: 0°, 36°, 72°, 108°, 144°, 180°, which is enough if each mark is used to draw a faint diameter.
- Dodecagon – mark: 0°, 30, 60°, 90°, 120°, 150°, 180°, which is enough if each mark is used to draw a faint diameter.

Explain how a hexagon can be drawn without the use of a protractor:

- Draw a circle of any radius but keep the compasses set to that measurement once drawn.
- Put the point of the compasses anywhere on the circumference and draw a tiny arc to cross the circumference the radius distance away.
- Put the compasses point exactly on the centre of the 'cross' thus formed and make a further arc on the circumference in the same direction.
- Continue around the circle until the final arc crosses the original compass point.
- Join the points made to reveal the hexagon.
- If the arcs are continued through from side to side, they should each pass exactly through the centre and, when all are drawn, a rather pleasing floral design is produced.

KEY AREA
Geometric
design

RESOURCES
Pencils and paper
Rulers

GROUP SIZE
Any

IDEA
91

DESIGNER LINE

This activity has endless possibilities. The concept is simple but it promotes accuracy and dexterity in measurement and drawing. Every child will finish up with an original design. It works especially well with upper KS2 but it can also be very successful in Years 3 and 4.

Demonstrate the method for the children to follow:

o Make a straight line of dots exactly 1cm apart right across a piece of A4 or A5 paper. The line can be horizontal, vertical or diagonal but, for the purposes of demonstration, it is best vertical and roughly central.

o Make a further dot at random anywhere in the open space on one side of the line of dots, preferably not too near them.

o Join this single dot to each of those in the line. Accuracy is important in order to gain the best effect from the finished result. Demonstrate holding the ruler against the pencil fixed at the single point. Carefully move the ruler until it is aligned to a dot on the line.

o When all the lined dots are joined to the single dot, choose an open space for another, either on the same side of the line or on the opposite side.

o There is no set number of outside dots to use and not all of the lined dots need to be used with them.

o When two or more dots are used on the same side of the line then a decision has to be made. The drawn line can stop when it meets a line already there, or cross it. It can look rather muddled if it simply crosses but very effective if crossing alternately in some way, e.g. creating a broken/dashed line. Whatever the decision, the ruler must be set in line with the dots. The choice is when to stop and start the pencil along that alignment.

o Colouring is optional but it can mar the overall effect of a well-drawn design. If colours are to be used, restrict this to two. Careful shading in monochrome makes a good finish.

○ Discourage the children from turning their design into a more representational picture by including freehand lines or neglecting the alignment of the dots. They might, however, want to give a title to their design as an indication of what it represents to them.

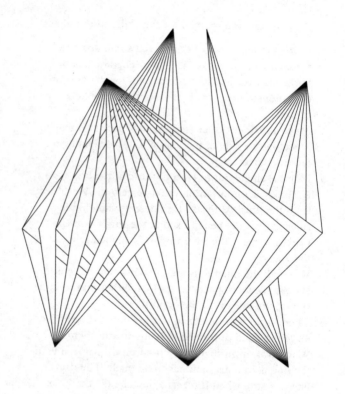

KEY AREA
2D
shapes/parallel
lines

RESOURCES
Pencils
A5 paper
Rulers
Card
Scissors
Masking tape
Colouring
pencils
(optional)

GROUP SIZE
Any

IDEA

92

SHAPES ON PARALLEL LINES

This activity reinforces the concept of parallel lines and presents an artistic angle on 2D shapes.

○ Children draw a large 2D shape, such as a kite, on a piece of card and cut it out.
○ Using a coiled piece of masking tape, they fix the card shape to a piece of plain A5 paper.
○ On another piece of the card, a curve is drawn, starting from a straight edge. The children should cut smoothly along the curve to give a template one straight edge and one curved edge.
○ The straight edge of the template is then abutted to one of the sides of the stuck-down shape, and children draw along the curve.
○ More curves are traced from the edge, moving the template against the straight sides as they go. The same template can be used for all sides of the shape or the children can alter the curve as they wish.
○ If the design is to be coloured, this should be done while the card shape is still fixed in place. This will ensure a sharp clear edge to the final shape.
○ Finally, the card shape is removed.

DIFFERENTIATION
○ Use shape templates for those who are unable to draw or cut out a shape accurately.

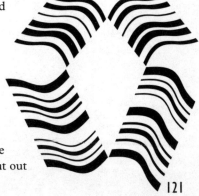

IDEA 93

SHAPE UP!

KEY AREA
2D and 3D
shape

RESOURCES
Blank cards
Paper and pencils

GROUP SIZE
Teams of pairs
or threes

This is a guessing game for KS2.

o Prepare a set of cards by writing the names of a 2D
  or 3D shape on each card.
o Shuffle the cards and place them in a pile face down.
o Players should be in teams of two or three.
o Each team nominates a member to look at the top
  card without letting on to their teammates what it is.
o On a signal these players draw the shape for their
  team. The first team to guess the shape correctly
  wins.
o Continue the game with team members taking turns
  to draw.

DIFFERENTIATION
Vary the complexity of the shapes used.

KEY AREA
Shape

RESOURCES
Drawing
instruments
Paper and pencils

GROUP SIZE
Works well with
pairs or small
collaborative
groups

IDEA
94

This KS2 activity is open-ended and can be widely
developed.

Set the task to present a study of quadrilaterals,
leaving content and presentation to the children, within
as many – or as few – parameters as you wish. This kind
of investigation is well suited to homework assignments.
The internet is a good source of inspiration and ideas.

Some suggested areas of content:

o The range of different quadrilaterals, drawn and
  named accurately: square, rectangle/oblong, rhombus,
  parallelogram, kite, delta, trapezium, irregular.
o The properties of individual shapes.
o Investigation of the angles.
o Designs drawn from a selected quadrilateral or a
  combination of more than one.
o Illustrations of quadrilaterals in the environment.
o Tessellations.

DIFFERENTIATION
Vary the expectations of the range and complexity
presented.

THE GREAT QUADRILATERAL INVESTIGATION

TETRAHEDRON

KEY AREA
3D shape

RESOURCES
Card
Rulers
Pencils
Scissors
Art materials
(optional)

GROUP SIZE
Any

KS2 children can generally see how cubes and cuboids can be produced from nets and they make them proficiently. The tetrahedron is often overlooked but it is actually easy to make and, with care, children can draw the template themselves.

Demonstrate the method, starting with a large equilateral triangle drawn either as described in Idea 90 or Idea 98 or as follows:

o A horizontal line, say, 20cm long, is drawn towards the bottom of an A4 piece of card.
o Mark the centre and draw a faint perpendicular line up from the mark, also about 20cm.
o Measure 20cm from one end of the horizontal baseline to the perpendicular line and draw that side.
o Complete the triangle.
o Mark the halfway points of each side.
o Join the halfway points to make a smaller equilateral triangle inside the large one. Dot these lines to indicate they are to be folded.

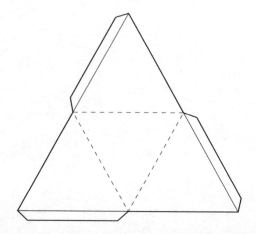

- There are now two smaller triangle sides on each large side, and alternate short sides must have a tab drawn on the outside for gluing the final shape together.
- Cut out the large triangle, remembering to cut around the tabs also.
- Score along the sides of the central triangle and along the folding edge of the tabs.
- If the shape is to be decorated, this should be done before folding and gluing.
- If the shape is to be hung, a coil of thread can be stuck into one of the apexes before folding and gluing.
- When ready, fold along the scored line and glue the tabs to the inside.

KEY AREA
Area and
perimeter

RESOURCES
Squared paper
Colouring
pencils

GROUP SIZE
Pairs

Try this game with KS2 children.

○ Players draw a 4 × 4 grid on 1cm squared paper and each chooses a different colour to use.
○ Players take turns to fill in a square anywhere on the grid. This should soon evolve into a strategy rather than merely random colouring.
○ When all the squares are coloured the area for each colour will be the same, as the players have had an equal number of turns.
○ Players calculate the perimeters of the shape or shapes they have made by counting. The highest total perimeter length wins the game.

DIFFERENTIATION
A 4 × 4 grid is about the smallest which can be used. Use larger grids as a challenge.

IDEA

97

LEAFY AREA

Take advantage of autumn and investigate leaf area.

o Ask the children to make a collection of leaves of different shapes and sizes, taking appropriate hygiene precautions. Recently fallen leaves are best.

o They select a leaf, place it on squared paper and draw round it.

o The leaf is put to one side and the squares within the drawn outline are counted. Part squares more than half-size count as one but part squares less than half-size are not counted.

o The species of the leaves and their respective areas can be displayed on a chart.

ADDITIONAL IDEAS

o Discuss how an estimation of total leaf area of a given tree might be attempted.

o Make a collective bar chart graph of leaf area, plotting groups of area, say, $2-10cm^2$, $11-20cm^2$, $21-30cm^2$ and so on against the number of leaves in the respective categories.

VARIATION

Try a similar process for an investigation of the area of body parts, if the children are willing. Simply draw around, on 1cm squared paper, the foot, a hand, a projected silhouette of the head in profile, or the whole body on the floor.

DIFFERENTIATION

o For the youngest children, collected leaves can be arranged in order of size.

KEY AREA
Shape

RESOURCES
Compasses
Rulers
Pencils
Plain paper
Protractors
(optional)

GROUP SIZE
Any

TRIANGLES FROM COMPASSES

This is geometry for upper KS2. Demonstrate how to construct triangles using compasses and allow practice at using a pair of compasses to measure distances between two or more points.

EQUILATERAL
○ Draw a baseline, any length.
○ Set the compasses to that length.
○ Place the point of the compasses at each end of the baseline in turn and make an arc in the open space above the centre, making sure the arcs cross.
○ Join each end of the baseline to the centre of the arc.

ISOSCELES
○ Draw a baseline, any length.
○ Set the compasses at a length different from the baseline.
○ Place the point of the compasses at each end of the baseline in turn and make an arc in the open space above the centre, making sure the arcs cross.
○ Join each end of the baseline to the centre of the arc.

SCALENE
○ Draw a baseline, any length.
○ Set the compasses at a length different from the baseline.
○ Place the point of the compasses at one end of the baseline and make an arc in the open space above.
○ Set the compasses at a length different from both these sides.
○ Place the point of the compasses at the other end of the baseline and make an arc in the open space above, making sure the arcs cross.
○ Join each end of the baseline to the centre of the arc.

RIGHT-ANGLED

With this one the sides need to be in the ratio 3:4:5.

o Draw a baseline, 8cm in length.
o Set the compasses at 6cm.
o Place the point of the compasses at one end of the baseline and make an arc in the open space immediately above that end.
o Set the compasses at 10cm.
o Place the point of the compasses at the other end of the baseline and make an arc to cross the first arc.
o Join each end of the baseline to the centre of the arc.

STRETCHING AND ENLARGING

KEY AREA
Shape/
coordinates

RESOURCES
Squared paper
Rulers
Pencils

GROUP SIZE
Any

This is an upper KS2 investigation of shape. For this example, an irregular pentagon is used. New shapes can be superimposed in a different colour on existing ones, or separate graphs produced.

○ Ask the children to draw x and y axes on squared paper, numbering the lines 0–fullest extent.

○ The corners of the shape are plotted: (2,2) (6,2) (6,5) (4,7) (2,5), and the sides drawn, thus producing a pentagon.

○ To stretch the shape horizontally, the value of x is doubled, giving in this example: (4, 2) (12, 2) (12, 5) (8, 7) (4, 5).

○ To stretch the shape vertically, the original value of y is doubled, giving in this example: (2, 4) (6, 4) (6, 10) (4, 14) (2, 10).

○ To enlarge the shape, the original values of both x and y are doubled, giving in this example: (4, 4) (12, 4) (12, 10) (8, 14) (4, 10).

○ Discuss the relative areas and perimeters of the shapes produced.

○ Discuss the effects of trebling, quadrupling and halving the values of x and y.

KEY AREA	RESOURCES	GROUP SIZE
Shape	Rulers	Any
	Pencils	
	Plain paper	
	Colouring	
	pencils	
	(optional)	

IDEA

100

SIMPLY TESSELLATION

This provides an easy way to produce tessellating parallelograms in a pleasing design, developing drawing accuracy.

○ Starting near the top, children draw two horizontal lines across a sheet of plain paper by using both sides of the ruler while holding it firmly in the same position.
○ The ruler is then aligned along the lower line and a third horizontal line is drawn.
○ Children continue drawing horizontal lines in this way to the bottom of the paper.
○ Starting from the left, the ruler is set at an angle across the top pair of horizontal lines and both sides of the ruler are drawn in *only* from line to line.
○ The ruler is then aligned along the second angled line in and a third angled line parallel to it is drawn.
○ This process is continued across the top two horizontal lines giving a series of parallelograms.

131

○ To make a second row of parallelograms the ruler must be carefully aligned. It should be angled in the opposite direction from those in the first row and *exactly* between the end points of the parallelograms above.

○ The parallel lines are continued across the second row.

○ The ruler direction is alternated as each row is drawn down the sheet of paper.

○ Shading or colouring the design is optional.